# The Model's Handbook

Or

## How to find and trap a modeling (or acting) assignment

2nd Edition

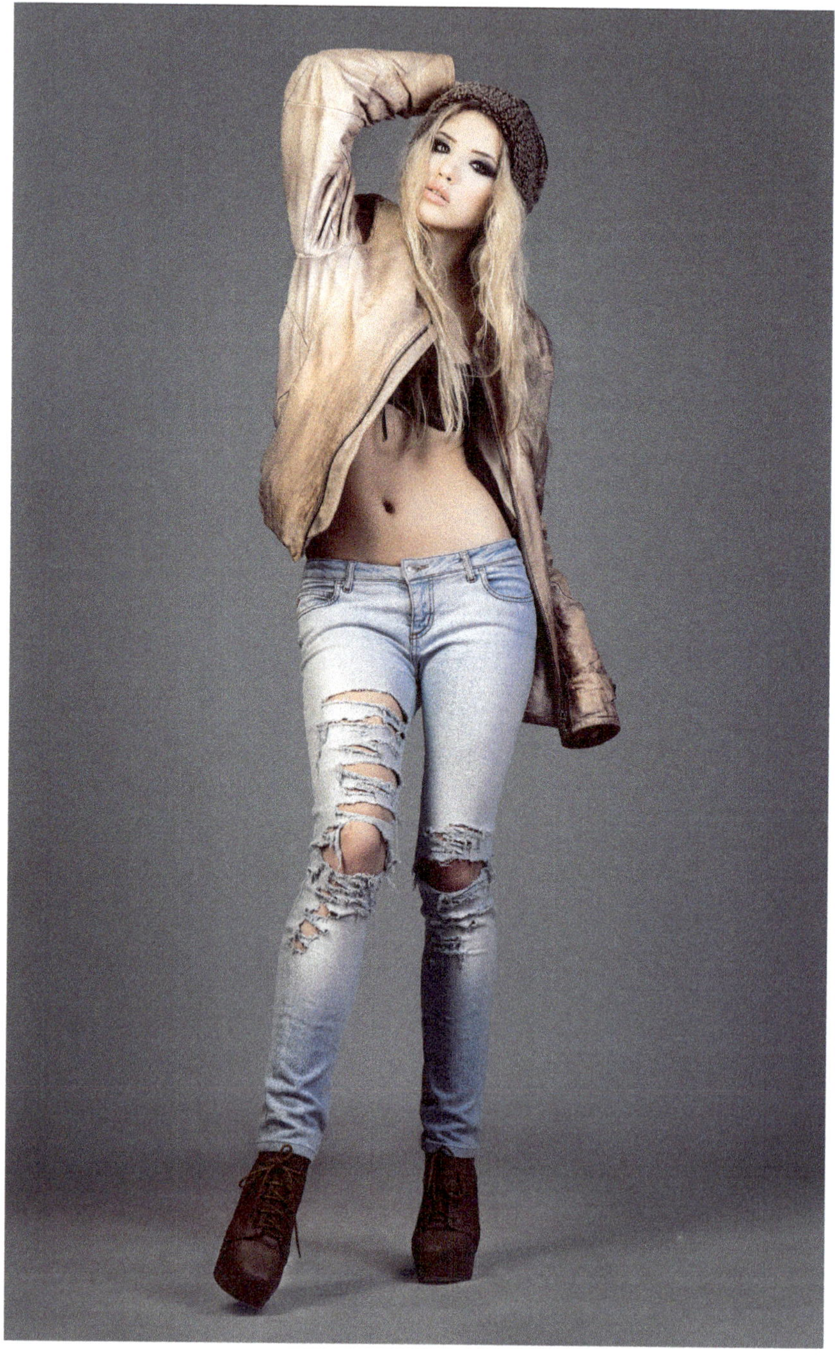

# The Model's Handbook

Or

How to find and trap a
modeling (or acting)
assignment

2nd Edition

---

William Robert Gately

published by
Brandt Media
Phoenix, AZ 85107

First Printing: 1982

Revised Second Edition First Printing 2014

**ISBN: 978-0-9862815-0-1**

Ordering Information:

Special discounts are available on quantity purchases by corporations, associations, educators, and others. For details, contact the publisher at the email address below.

published by
Brandt Media
Phoenix, AZ 85107
http://brandtmedia.wix.com/james-b-brandt#!the-models-handbook/cwzg

brandtmedia@yahoo.com

# Table of Contents

**Why should I read this book?** ........ vi

**1 THE TOOLS** ........ 1
- PHOTOGRAPHS ........ 1
- PORTFOLIO ........ 5
- COMPOSITES ........ 7
- THE RESUME ........ 14
- POSTCARDS ........ 15

**2 THE ECONOMICS** ........ 19
- THE HIGH COST OF ADVERTISING ........ 19
- HOW MUCH ARE YOU WORTH? ........ 22

**3 FINDING THE ASSIGNMENT** ........ 28
- ADVERTISING AGENCIES ........ 28
- VIDEO PRODUCERS ........ 30
- CASTING AGENTS ........ 33
- WHAT CASTING DIRECTORS WANT ........ 40
- TALENT AGENTS ........ 43
- TALENT MANAGERS ........ 50
- OTHER LEADS ........ 52
- DO IT YOURSELF ........ 57

**4 MAKING THE PITCH** ........ 60
- INTERVIEWS ........ 60
- THE AUDITION ........ 62
- GRAMMAR ........ 64
- APPEARANCE ........ 68
- WHAT TO DO AFTER THE AUDITION ........ 70
- THE POWER OF NO ........ 71

**5 ON ASSIGNMENT** ........ 73
- THE TIME CLOCK ........ 73
- BRING IT ALL – AND THEN SOME ........ 74

**6 BETWEEN ASSIGNMENT SURVIVAL** ........ 77
- THE REGULAR JOB ........ 77
- OTHER SOURCES ........ 78

**7 LEGALITIES** ........ 81
- COPYRIGHT ........ 81
- MODEL RELEASES ........ 82
- BUYOUTS, RESIDUALS,& ROYALTIES ........ 84
- TAXES ........ 87

**8 DO IT** ........ 89

**Photo Credits** ........ 91

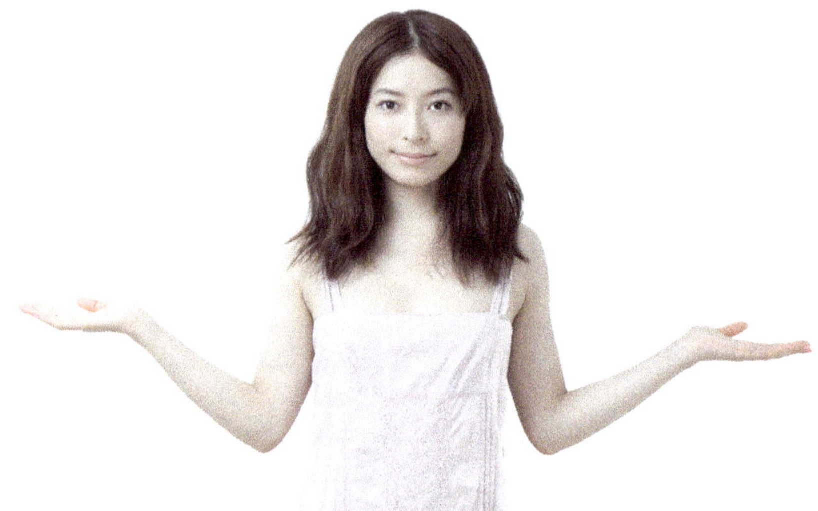

## Why should I read this book?

It's a hard, cold world in front of the photographic camera. The competition is rough, rude, cutthroat, and downright nasty. There are thousands of models looking for their big break and they all seem to be looking in the same place and at the same time as you. Some make the grade; most do not. In all honestly, it is not a matter of looks or blind luck (at least, not totally) but more a matter of how you see your opportunities, how you make your own luck, and how you use the luck you make.

That is the foundation of this book: how to create good luck. There are certain steps that will help the talented and conscientious model build a profitable career. There is no amount of advice that will produce work for the model, unless the model acts on that advice. That is your job: to take what has been gathered and compile here and make use of it. Unless you make the effort, you will always be a dreamer and never accomplish anything.

What I can do, and will do here, is tell you the secrets which separate the amateur from the novice, the novice from the professional. Even if you are handed a golden opportunity for your first modeling job, it will end then and there if you do not have the skills needed to fill out a full portfolio. It is the extremely rare case where the door opens and recognition floods in and that momentum can be maintained untouched, even with today's Internet.

Let me be absolutely clear: modeling is a sales job. You are selling YOUR BRAND every minute of the day. Your Brand? Yep. You are your own Brand: your name, your face, your skill, that package that is uniquely you. It is a fragile construct, this brand. If it slips, you lose your marketability. You stop working. You are the girl - or boy - who never was or who once was way back in the day... sometime the day is just last week.

You will work hard to build your Brand, harder to promote it, and harder still to keep from tarnishing it. While social media, which we will discuss later in this text, can reach hundreds of thousands of people with your image with a few clicks, it can also shatter that image just as fast.

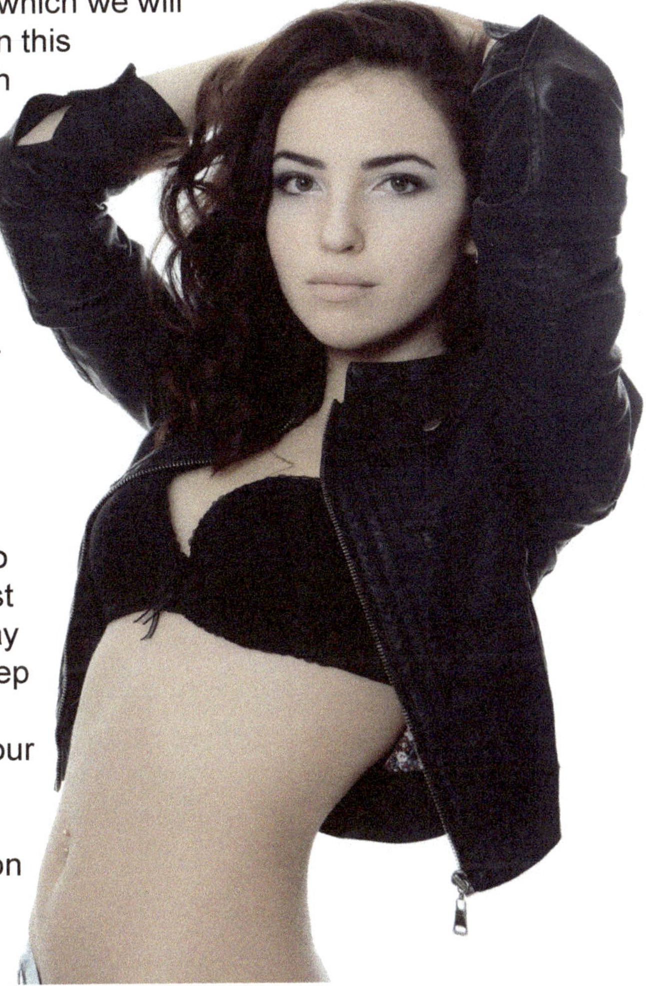

The following pages will tell you how to make your first impression pay off, how to keep it viable, and how to turn your heart's desire into a profitable profession rather than a costly hobby.

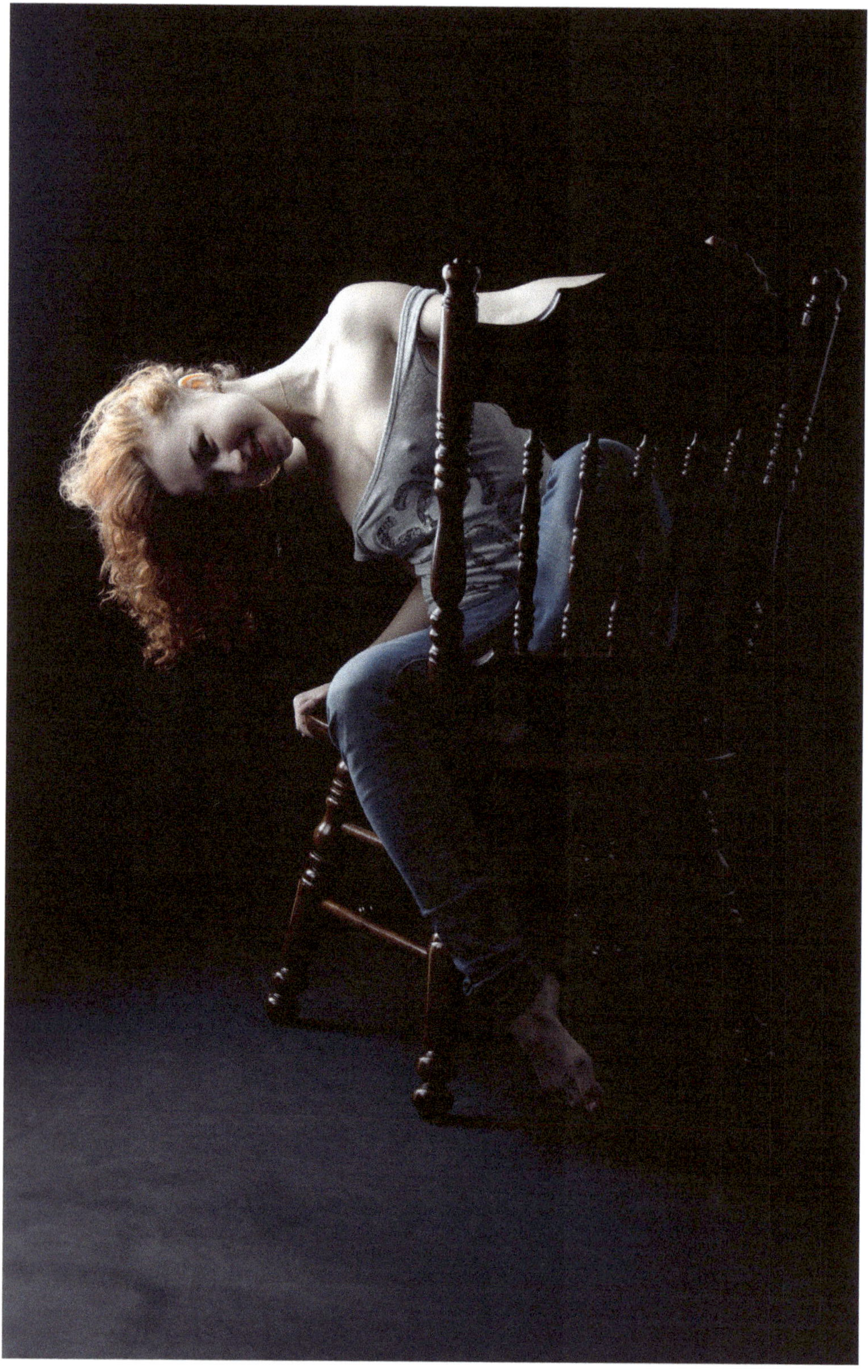

# I THE TOOLS

## PHOTOGRAPHS

The most important tool a model has is her portfolio. The photographs it contains are her calling cards and her proof of performance. Almost every employer will ask the model for a sample of her work (her portfolio) and to leave copies of her photographs (her composites) for their file. In every case, these samples must be of the absolute best quality. Here is not the place to skimp with finances - even though we will talk about how to get them for (mostly) free.

If the photographic quality is poor, the employer will think that the model is not concerned with quality and she will not be seriously considered for the prospective assignment. A well-done model's portfolio can launch an average looking girl into the spotlight... if she does it right.

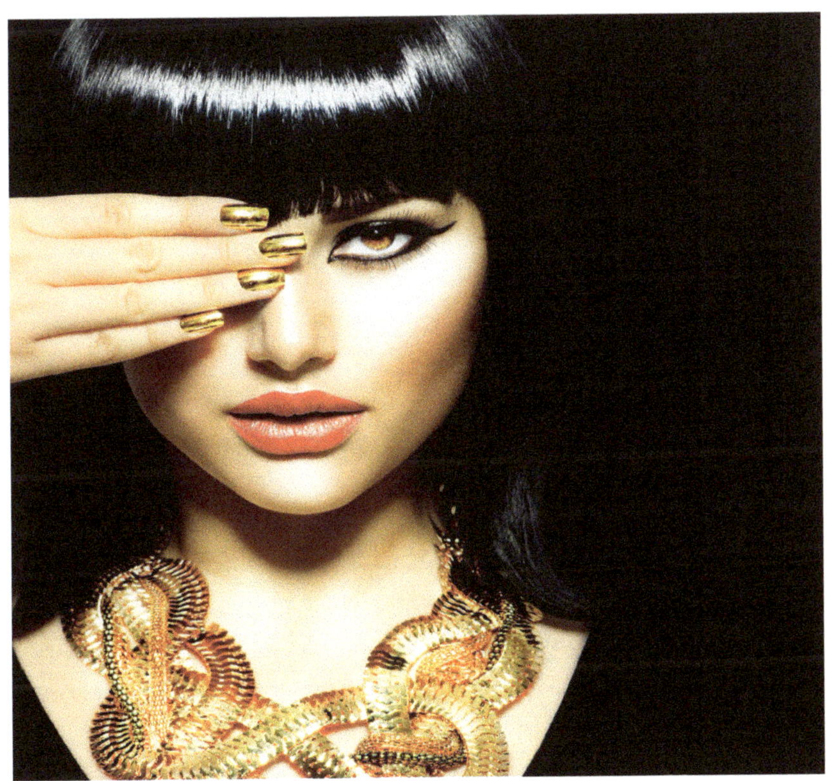

Because the model must maintain the best possible quality with her photographic work, a professional photographer is usually the only choice acceptable, though there are talented amateurs who can do credible work. A professional photographer may cost between $200 and $800 for the shoot alone (please note, however, that higher price does not guarantee higher quality) plus the cost of the photographs ordered. If the model shops around, she can usually find a good photographer in the $200-$300 range who offers prints at a fair price.

Prints are vital even in this digital age since you need something to show a client face-to-face. You will also want digital copies of any work you pay for in hi-def. These are invaluable in today's Internet market and can make printing headshots and composites easier.

***Tip: Always get both paper prints and digital copies of your photos.***

The type of photographer the model chooses is also very important. There are many excellent portrait photographers across the country. However, these photographers may not be able to photograph the model in the poses she needs for her portfolio/composites. Modeling photography takes a special type of photographic technique and requires a special photographic eye. A good portfolio photographer will not make the model look like she was posing for a portrait, a men's magazine, or a snap shot.

The model's photographs should represent the model in attitudes associated with the advertising field. It is the advertising industry that provides the pay for most modeling assignments and this is the style of photography employers will expect to see in the model's portfolio. Other styles are not acceptable, not in a portfolio.

I worked with a lovely girl in her early twenties. We discussed what was needed in a portfolio. I thought she understood the look we wanted, but when she came back with a folder full of portraits, it was back to square one. If the photograph looks like it was taken in a department store photo shop, it will hurt more than help. She had the requisite number of different looks, different outfits, and different poses, but they were all what you would expect from a portrait photographer who shoots kids or families as opposed to a commercial photographer. Even head-shots need to have the look and feel of commercial work. Without that, your application is trashed.

If the model has a friend who can do adequate technical work and who can properly photograph the model,

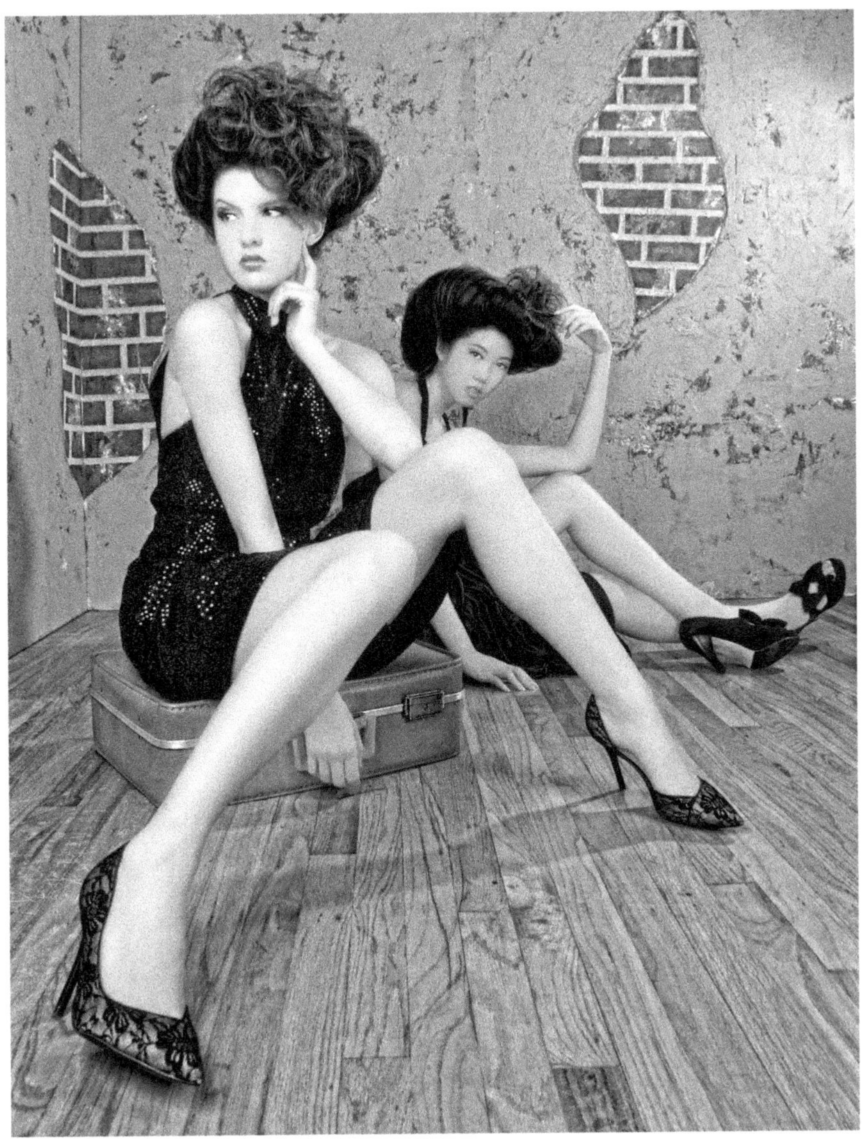

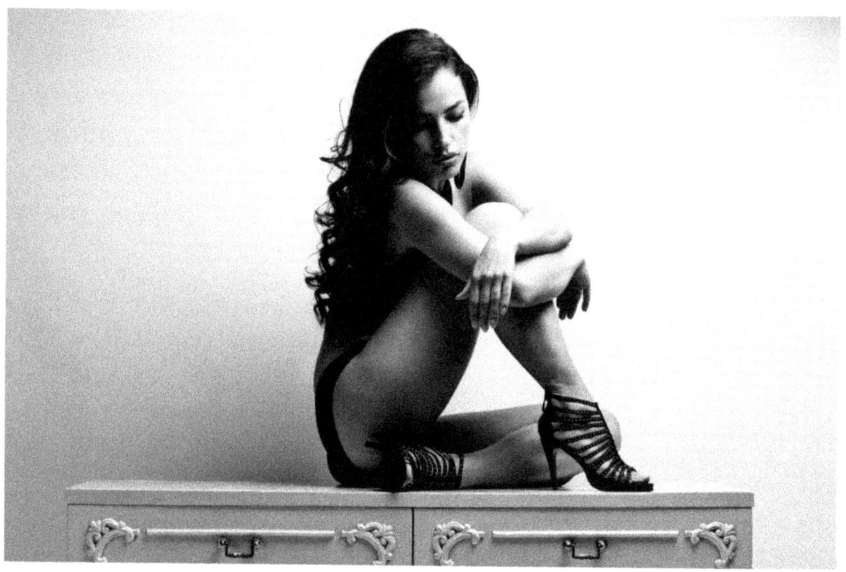

then it is certainly permissible to work with the talented amateur in the early (and broke) days of the model's career. However, the model should be aware that it may take much, much longer to produce the proper number and styles of prints required under these conditions. It may also be very frustrating and upsetting to keep re-taking the photographs because the photographer was unable to focus properly or could not capture the proper pose or lighting.

An alternative to using a friend with the nifty camera is to call around the commercial photography studios and see if anyone is planning on doing a test session with new equipment, in an exotic location, or just to sharpen their own skills. You will trade time for prints. But be absolutely sure that the release you sign stipulates that the photos are for the photographer's use only and may not be sold or used in a commercial manner without compensation and approval. If the photographer is being paid for his work, then so should you, even if he does not sell the photo immediately.

Before deciding on any photographer, insist on seeing the photographer's portfolio. Compare quality and compare prices. Even if you are not an expert, you should still be able to recognize a difference in the quality of the work you are viewing. By now, you should also have a handful of clippings from magazines of images you would like to emulate. If the photographer's work is not up to that quality, move to another photographer. Show the clips to the photographer; perhaps they will inspire him to create the right kind of images.

***Tip: Photographers' styles differ with each individual. Find one you like, especially if you are paying.***

If possible, try to talk to other models that have used a photographer you are considering. It is very important to know how long it takes the photographer to deliver the promised prints, his relative quality, and how he behaves on a shoot. This is important even if you are doing a trade deal. If it takes months for the photographer to deliver photos, then you have wasted your time. Also, ask about the photographer's willingness to do a re-shoot if the original shooting is unacceptable. If it is the fault of the photographer, he should be willing to re-shoot without charging or, at the very least, charging only for supplies.

Be very careful in your choice, but be willing to pay the price for good quality work. It is a good photographic base from which all things will spring.

## PORTFOLIO

Model portfolios consist of 6-12 8x10 or 11x14 black and white and 2-4 color prints contained in a proper presentation case. The portfolio case may be purchased at most art supply houses. Do not use a notebook binder!

The model should have at least one 11x14-color photograph, but a full color portfolio is not recommended. Black and white photographs are the standard and some people believe they are a truer representation of the model than are color prints. Since many advertising photos are still printed in black and white, a good representation of black and white images is required, even when the portfolio is predominantly color.

Color photography is often striking (if properly printed) and may be used in a larger percentage of the portfolio if it is not cost prohibitive. With digital printing having reached photographic quality for a very low cost, price is seldom a prohibiting factor with using color in a portfolio. The print size most recommended for a color close-up is 11x14. The facial close-up, when enlarged to 11x14, is almost the same size as the face in real life. If you are just using one in color, this should be a traditional head-shot with light make-up. Do not get sucked into something exotic with wild hair and "fashion model" make-up. The hiring agent is looking to see what *you* look like, not to judge the work of a hair/make-up artist or to see the whacked-out fantasies of a pubescent photographer.

***Tip: Find out what everyone else is doing... and do something completely different!***

Always insist on top quality photographic printing. You want custom printing, not machine printing, unless the prints are from a digital source and color balanced and touched up before printing on a high end photo printer. You should also insure that a fair number of black and white shots are taken with any shoot (regardless of your personal preference) because sooner or later, someone will want some and black and white prints always develop better from black and white negatives than from color negatives. Even with

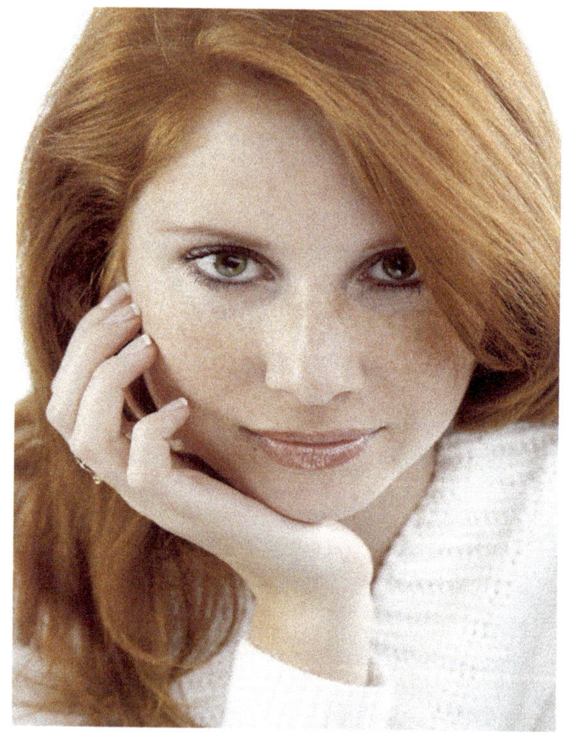

digital techniques, if the photographer is competent with black and white film, these produce better photos than a color image printed as a grayscale photo.

***Tip: Part of your Portfolio should be YOU! Create a unique look, don't do what everyone else is doing, and have a few outstanding photos that the casting director calls "Awesome" so you don't ever have to use the word.***

When you do begin to work, you should put "tear sheets" of the work you do in your portfolio. These are samples of your work that you rip out of magazines or newspapers in which your photograph appears. Tear sheets make excellent letters of recommendation and eliminate doubts about your claimed experience. Many models make the mistake of not asking for tear sheets or a copy of the publication or video as part of the release requirements. If you are sitting in a casting office talking about a shoot for the local Ford dealer, all you have is talk with no proof. For those familiar with online gaming, the phrase "if you don't have a screenshot it didn't happen" has as much validity in the professional modeling world as it does with people who live their life in online fantasy.

## COMPOSITES

Composites are vital tools for the model. Whenever she applies for a job, the person doing the interview will forget how she looks within 24 hours. Or less if it was a large casting call. The casting agent may very well forget you the instant you walk out of the room. The casting agent will never be able to properly describe the model to another person or client. Try it some time. Describe your best friend to someone who doesn't know them.

Chances are excellent the mental image you create and reality are vastly different. You should always leave a photograph at the interview. There is no other possible way that you can keep your name and face in the casting agent's mind after you leave the offices.

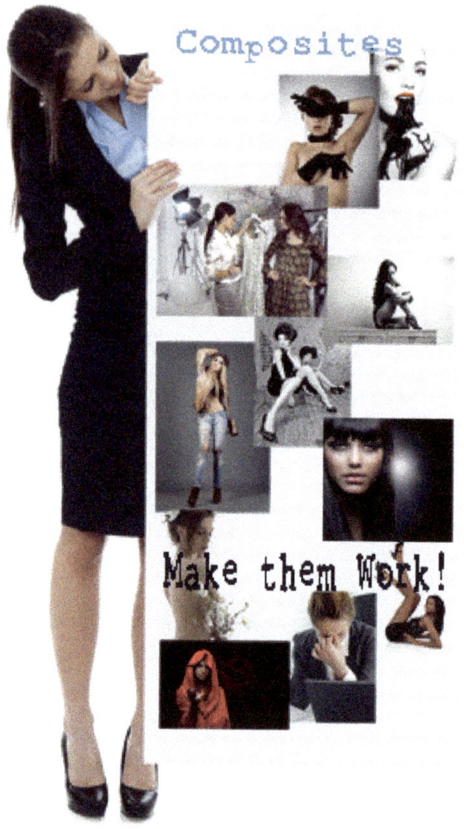


***Tip: Always leave your most current work. The photograph you leave must be with the look you have now. Leaving something older can eliminate your chances of landing the job.***

Composites should be no larger than 8½x11. Some are smaller, but experience has shown that the composites smaller then 8x10 often get lost in the shuffle. It is advisable to choose a size that will fit into readily available envelopes. Each composite should have from 3 to 5 photographs of the model and images should be of a size large enough to be easily viewed.

These are, of course, black and white photographs, though the cost for color printing has come down enough that one side of color is not outrageously expensive. It is OK if the composite is designed to be folded into a smaller size. Just have flat ones to hand one out at an audition that stays open and flat.

Since composites are generally printed on offset presses, the quality can vary greatly from printer to printer. Never accept "quick print" photocopier quality. Never accept work which uses less than a 110-line screen. A 150-line screen is a touch more expensive but well worth the price.

Composites are your calling card. If you do not pay close attention to the paper stock, the ink, the lay-out, the graphic design, the screening, and the scoring, then you will be leaving a sloppy, counter-productive reminder of your visit. Poor quality may save some money now but it will cost you much more in lost wages later.

Remember that advertising agencies deal with the printing on a daily basis. They know a good quality job – and they know a bad quality job. A printer might fool you but you will never fool the hiring manager at an ad agency. Even if you are handing your prints to someone who knows nothing about printing, they will know the difference between acceptable quality and cheap reproductions after just a few days shuffling through stacks of resumes.

Shop for the best price, but also for the best quality. Do not just take the lowest bidder. Look for quality discounts with the right quality. While 250 composites might cost

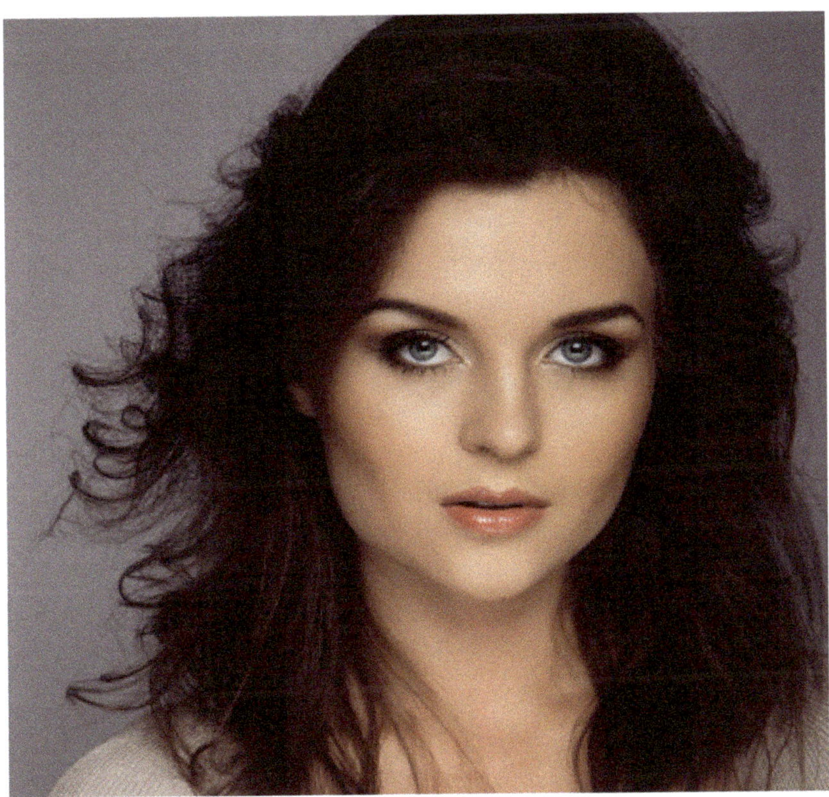

$200, 500 may only cost $250. Do not buy over 500 – most people change long before they can use that many composites. Unless you are planning a massive mailing campaign, the smaller number is fine.

Stick with a good paper stock. You may use coated or non-coated, but do not use textured or off-white papers. Make sure the paper is heavy enough to prevent "bleeding through" if you print a 2-sided composite. That means that the photo on the back does not show through on the front. I recommend 100# text or #80 cover, coated or matte white.

If the composite is designed to fold, have it scored - but not folded - by the printer. This makes folding neater and more professional looking. Scored composites are fine when flat. It is not necessary to fold the composite unless you plan on mailing it in a small envelope. Composites are most often stapled flat on a resume and/or a casting sheet provided by the casting agent. If scored they may be folded and mailed.

***Tip: Composites should have at least one headshot, a "character" shot (something unusual), and two full-length shots, one of which is in something that shows off the legs and figure.***

Models may also opt to have "headshots" printed. These are an 8x10 reproduction of a close up. This is in addition to a composite, not a substitute as some models believe. Actors may get away with just a headshot, but models need to show their versatility on paper where an acting audition today is most often video recorded. The composite, while containing close ups, will also have full length and body shots included. The headshot is just that: a generic shot of your face and not a character shot; this should be something with character but it needs to show a clear shot of your face without stage make-up (or make up that is not intrusive). Video producers usually prefer headshots.

This is a tool you use to help keep your name and face on the casting agent's mind, so it is important that it shows you as you normally are, not in a character (unless, of course, you are marketing yourself only as a character)! You want the casting agent to recognize you when you walk in the room and the headshot should be the key to achieving that goal. The headshot is a valuable tool, especially if the resume is printed on the reverse side. Headshots should be printed in smaller quantities - normally 100 - and changed frequently.

One would hope the resume needs frequent updates, but you should also leave something every time you visit a potential client and it is best to leave something different than what you left at your previous visit. Stick with good paper stock for the headshot too. You may use coated or non-coated paper, but do not use textured or off-white papers.

Make sure the paper is heavy enough to prevent "bleed through" here as well, though 60# for single sided and 80# text for double usually OK. Don't worry if you don't understand the technical stuff - the printer will. A standard 8x10 photograph is acceptable and there are companies that will print 100 at reasonable prices.

I have interviewed models who presented headshots run off on a copier with their resume on the back. These usually went right into the reject file. If I am paying $20-100 an hour with a 4-hour minimum, I want someone who demonstrates professionalism and a concern for quality. Unscreened photo copies will never pass muster.

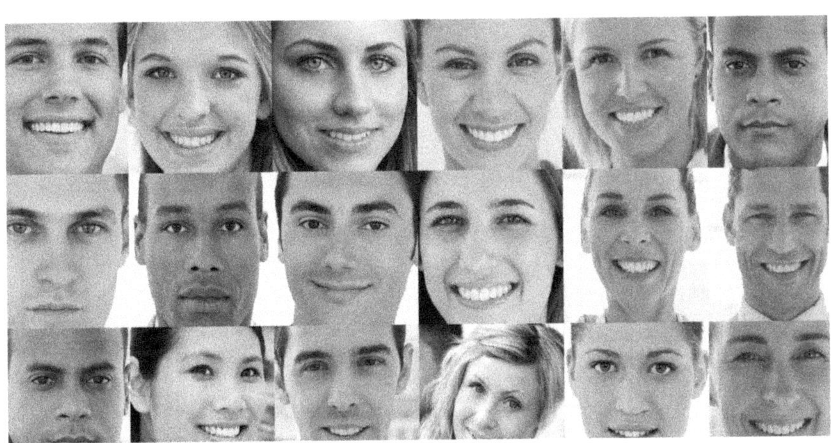

Many people think that a composite is enough ammunition for them to succeed. It is not. For some models in some markets, perhaps that is true if they are already well-known and established, but for most people, both composites and headshots are required. It is a matter of economics as well as presentation. Many composites include color printing and color composites are more expensive than black and white headshots. It is very costly to update a color composite as frequently as you can update black-and-white headshots.

Consider the "philosophy" behind headshots and composites: they are designed to be given away. They are considered expendable, so people who have no desire or need for a composite will still ask for one. Maybe they think you will feel bad if they do not ask, maybe they just want a photo for their wall, or maybe they are building a file for later use - and that last one is good for you. Whatever their motive, their request costs you money.

Look at the cost per-item of composites and headshots: which one is more expensive? Sometimes they differ by significant amounts. So you have an option: drop one - usually a composite - at an advertising agency or casting director, and drop the cheaper one for the cattle call, the casual contact, or the audition where variety is less important. While your initial printing investment may be a little larger, the materials last longer. If there is a call back or you visit the potential client at a later date, leave the other handout then.

The headshot can also serve as a resume sheet. Print headshots with your resume printed on the back. As a casting director for film and commercial work, I always preferred headshots with resumes printed on the back.

These are easier to handle for several reasons: they are all about the same size (8½x11 or 8x10, not the odd sizes that grace some of the more interesting and artistic composites designs); they are one sheet (as opposed to a composite with a resume stapled to it); and they are easier to track (less chance of individual elements becoming separated during handling).

However, when I cast for a client who is strictly print orientated, I have found that composites help me sell my choice better than just a headshot. Agency art directors are often interested a variety of looks and the model's physical characteristics.

Of course, the option to leave multiple copies, say a headshot/resume and a composite, always exists. This can be an effective sales tool if used intelligently. There is a subtle psychological advantage with a "spontaneous" offer to leave an extra composite with the headshot.

Headshots are usually printed in quantities of 100. It is expected that you will change that shot on a regular basis - this means every time you change your look. If you streak or tip your hair, it means a new headshot. If your hair has been cut or significantly longer now, a new headshot is required. A large number is more efficient when you are just entering the business and have a large number of photographers, art directors, casting directors to visit in a relatively short time. Men can occasionally justify a larger quantity than women since there "look" usually changes infrequently.

As you start working more, you will have an increasing variety of shots available, and changing the headshot gives you a reason to revisit your media contact. The excuse is to give them an updated headshot, but the real reason is that you know that making that personal contact is the best way to keep your name on their mind when a casting call comes around.

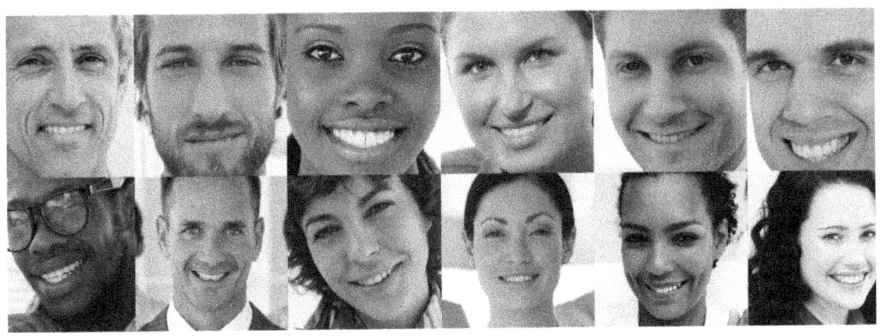

When ordering composites, look closely at paper size options. You will save money if you can "gang" several composites on one larger page and have them cut to size after printing. Talk to your printer about paper sizes and page layouts that will allow you to place the most number of composites per page.

Composites can be printed at any angle that permits easy printing. If you are at a conventional printer and not a copy store, the paper is usually in a much larger sheet and cut to size after printing. This cuts costs on larger runs.

## THE RESUME

Once the model has gained some experience, a resume should be compiled. Always put the most recent work first since it is usually only the first three or four entries that will be read by the interviewer. Keep it simple and short. You want to present the facts without confusing the casting director and you want him to be able to find the information quickly and easily. If you do not have experience, do not lie. The truth will show before the camera. Besides, people talk.

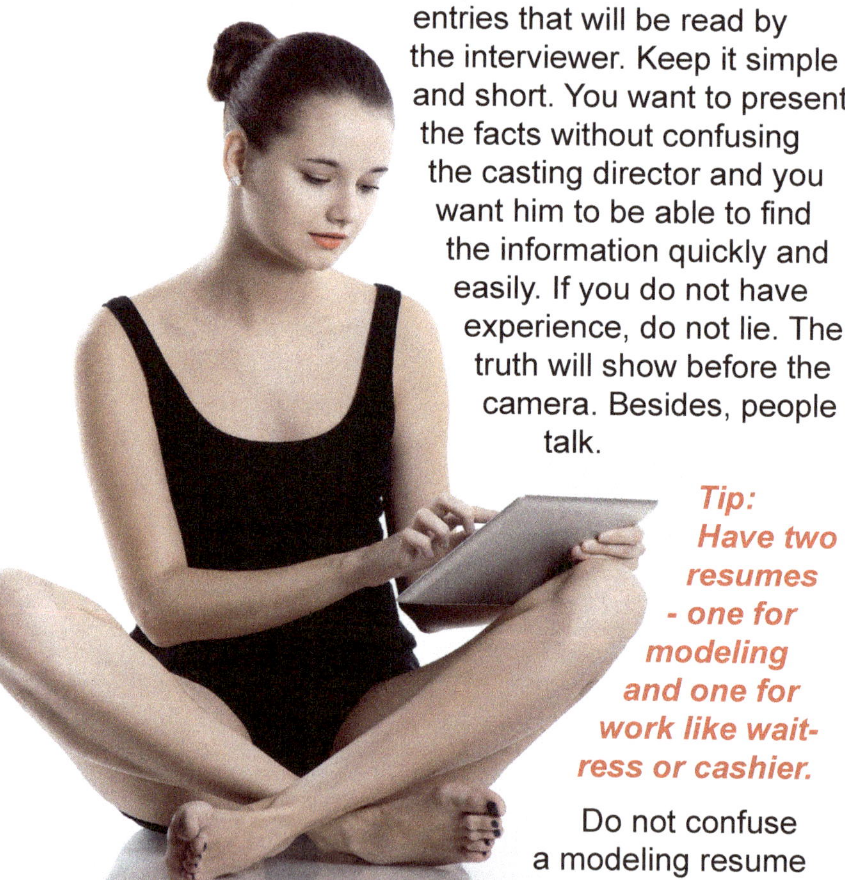

***Tip: Have two resumes - one for modeling and one for work like waitress or cashier.***

Do not confuse a modeling resume

with a job resume. Your modeling resume will contain vital statistics (measurements and clothing sizes), special abilities, union affiliations, and training. It is a more a credit list that an actual resume and need not contain more than the shoot, role, producer/photographer, and category.

Always type the resume or use a word processing program with a laser printer. NOTHING is handwritten these days. Use a standard font (Arial, Garamond, Times, or Calibri) that can easily be scanned. Always check and double check for spelling and typographical errors. Have others proofread your work… several times. It is amazing how often a mistake can slip past, and mistakes are very unprofessional.

***Tip: Your training and education section of your resume should always be growing!***

I cannot emphasize enough the need for honesty. It is too easy to verify credits. I have had models and actors come in with resumes and parts listed on projects I have produced - never seen them before. Quick shuffle out the door and word spreads.

I have had producers who knew about programs I produced and called me about a resume they received crediting work on that program. If it wasn't right, that person didn't work.

Once, there was an actress who appeared as a guest on a web series I was producing. She listed the part as a co-host. Wrong. I had a "man-on-the-street" actor in a documentary list himself as a co-host on a documentary. Sooner or later it will all come back and a reputation sticks.

## POSTCARDS

Some models have turned to post cards as an effective marketing tool. There are several ways to produce postcards. There are probably local printers who can take a good black and white card with a 150 line screen, print it on a good, coated card stock, cut, and package a few hundred postcards at a reasonable price.

There are also a half-dozen or so printers who advertise on a national basis that produce color postcards in quantities of 2500 that are reasonably priced. Color can have a tremendous impact and are readily noticed. The 2500 number makes sense if you live in LA or New York, perhaps Dallas, Atlanta, Miami, or any other large market with an active advertising community. It also makes sense in small communities or cities like Phoenix (which has a relatively poor advertising community) when you are sending out to both local and LA/NY casting agents and producers.

A postcard is a matter of personal taste, but to reap the most impact, one side should be only the photograph you are sending out, no text except - perhaps - a contact number printed over a small section of the photograph; but the picture needs to be outstanding and eye-catching. This is the one place where you can put the wild fashion photo and be effective. You want the card to be noticed and passed around and kept. If you are real lucky, someone will pin it to a note board in their cubical! (Wild, but nothing too sexy. The goal is to grab attention, not to become a pin-up girl!)

The backside should be a brief note. Something like: "Hi! I just wanted to share this photo from my recent portfolio shoot with (photographer). I look forward to working with you in the near future. Please feel free to call my agent at any time!" Keep the copy short, make sure there is a contact number, and keep it professional. It is OK here to use a script font. Or you can neatly hand print something more personal or personalized to the receiver - something different for photographers and producers, for example.

Postcards (which cost much more to mail than to print) need to be used judiciously, but I have known top models to send one out every few months. I am absolutely positive that this approach with an established model will

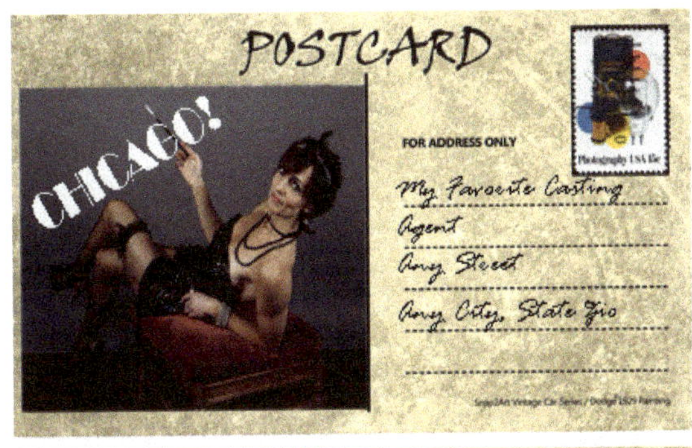


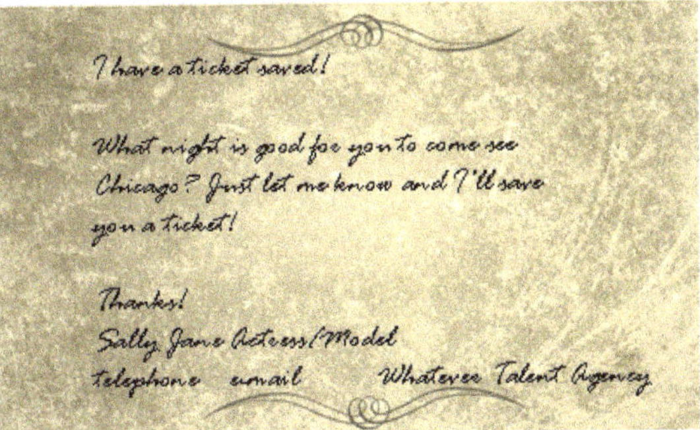


bring in much more work than the postage fees.

If you are new, you might want to wait until you have something major to boast about. It could be a new shoot or a new commercial. But there is also no reason not to send out postcards to announce a new look – shorter hair or your braces off your teeth – or to introduce yourself to the local casting agencies, ad agencies, and photographs prior to starting a door-to-door campaign with a personal introduction. Remember, too, that Black and white postcards can be as effective as color.

Many models are also purchasing web space, but I do not recommend this until you are somewhat established. Instead, look for free sites (like Wix or Weebly) that make building something easy and free. For both new and established models, there are portfolio sites available. They publish a series of photographs online that the casting agents can view at their leisure (Modelmayhem, Portfoliobox, Studioself, and foliohd are some popular choices, though there are others). These service providers have developed a site that is designed for portfolio presentation or talent registries and usually offer both free and premium services.

***Tip: A web presence can be used to show off more photos than a composite and can be updated with little or no cost more frequently than print work.***

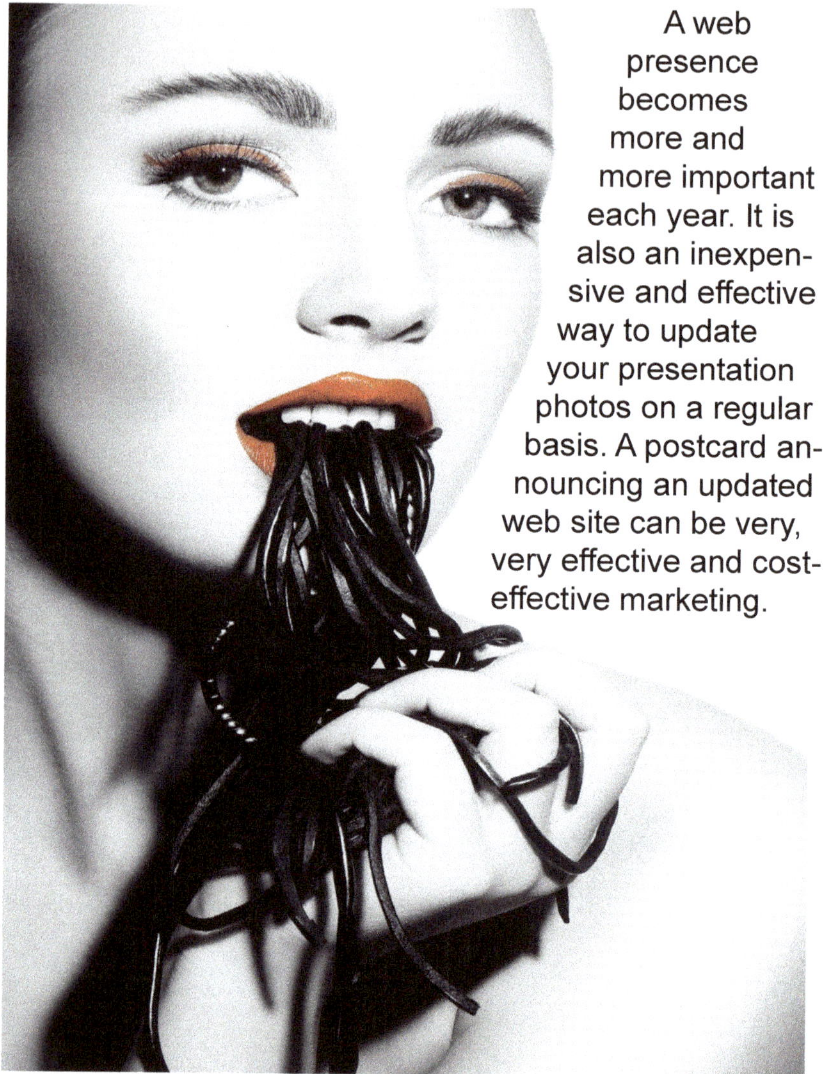

A web presence becomes more and more important each year. It is also an inexpensive and effective way to update your presentation photos on a regular basis. A postcard announcing an updated web site can be very, very effective and cost-effective marketing.

There is more on the Internet later in this book. However, one thing to remember: if nobody knows about your web site, it is worthless. You need to push people to your site relentlessly. We will get more into that later, but any web presence you have needs to be on your postcards, composites, headshots, resumes, and anything else you are making public in your search for modeling jobs.

# 2 THE ECONOMICS

## THE HIGH COST OF ADVERTISING

Before you even consider looking for a modeling job, it is important for you to recognize the financial obligations involved, especially on the advertiser's part. If you expect to be paid for your work (if you do not expect to be paid, do not model professionally), then you must provide a service which is not only satisfactory but makes money for your employer.

Consider the cost of making a local television commercial on a thirteen week placement contract.

| | |
|---|---|
| Talent fees, one model | $ 650 |
| Talent fees, Announcer | $ 450 |
| Production crew ($/day) | $3,500 |
| Editing and Mixing | $5,000 |
| Total production costs | $9,590 |

On top of the money spent on the production, the company must buy air time on television or cable. This can be very expensive if bought on prime time television or during the news; or it can be relatively cheap if purchased during a late, late, late show time slot or on local cable. In any case, most studies agree that the average amount of airtime purchased by local advertisers is close to 20 thousand dollars. When we use this figure as a basis, we see that the total production cost can run up from $29,590. Generally, considering special sets being constructed, special effects, titles and other superimpositions, copywriting, expendables, etc., that figure runs closer to $50 thousand.

What does all this mean? Simply this: you, as the model, are responsible for selling over one million dollars* of merchandise for the company to break even. No company with stay in business by just breaking even; it must make money. That means that the one or two days YOU are before the camera are very important to the advertiser. You must do your job very well or the company will lose money.

Should you care? After all, you have already been paid your initial talent fee. You most certainly should care! Some companies run a new add every two or three months. If you wish an opportunity to receive a steady paycheck from that company, you must sell their products. If you do not, you will not work for that company very often.

Consider, too, that if a commercial is successfully moving product, the client will keep running it in many cases. If you have been cast in a union - Screen Actors Guild (SAG) or American Federation of Television and Radio Artists (AFTRA) - commercial and did not take a buy-out offer, you receive a payment every time the commercial runs. I had a young actor land a spot in a Hubba Bubba Bubble Gum commercial. All he did was act surprised at the POP and dump a bucket of oats. His earnings and residuals during his last two years in high school paid for his move to Los Angeles and gave him the time he needed to establish himself in the industry. Never once did he ask if anyone wanted fries with their order!

It is your job as the model to sell the client's product. Period. You must always do the best you can. Why? That's easy. Think about the national ads you see on television every day. The least expensive cost over a million dollars to produce and the company is buying several million dollars worth of airtime. That makes your job even more demanding and the pay even better. Between a single day's work and two years of residuals on a normal run, even minimal exposure over a two year period can net the model over $70,000 for a single day's work.

For national magazine advertising, the figures are just as astounding. Most magazine rates are figured on the total reading audience. That means that ads run in high circulation magazines like *Seventeen, Cosmopolitan*, and *Playboy* will all cost about the same, or around one million dollars in production and space charges for a full-page color ad. That is BEFORE the consumer ever sees the ad. That means the company must sell approximately twenty million dollars of product to break even. That is one heck of a lot of eye shadow or diet shakes.

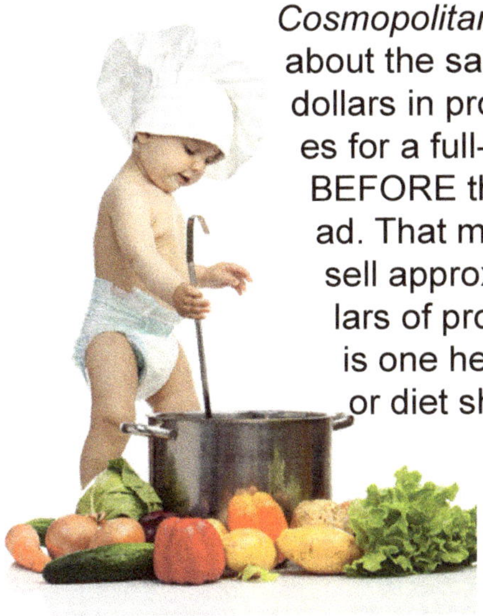

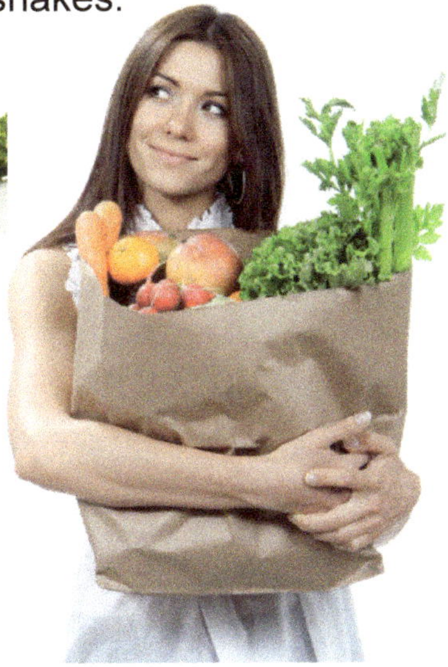

When you start modeling, it is easy to think of only the $20 or $30 an hour you might be making and to forget the purpose and your place in the total picture. This can lead to sloppy modeling. Always remember that someone, somewhere generally has a lot of money riding on your performance. Even if it is only a photographer trying to build up his portfolio, it is very easy for him to spend well over $200.00 in wholesale film costs, processing and miscellaneous charges for a day's shooting or countless hours at a computer if he is shooting digital. Photographic modeling is not inexpensive. You may only see the fun and glamour before the camera, but never forget that there is someone whose entire business and, perhaps, livelihood may be depending on your performance.

**This figure is based on a standard 5% advertising budget recommended for established business in most business management texts. To find the total break-even point of any ad, multiply the total cost by 20.*

## HOW MUCH ARE YOU WORTH?

Even as a beginner, you are worth SOMETHING. If a client is going to make money from the modeling you do, then you should ALWAYS be paid. As a novice, you may ask for less than professional, but always ask for something. If the producer develops the habit of paying in the beginning, it will be easier to receive professional wages when you deserve them.

Often it is very difficult for professional models to find good-paying jobs because there are so many models willing to work for free. Keep one simple rule in mind: if the client is going to use your image and efforts to make money then you should be paid.

Sometimes you may wish to work with a photographer who is an amateur with models and cannot afford to pay the $20 an hour minimum you ask. It is all right to work for this type of assignment as long as you know that the photographer is not going to sell the photographs

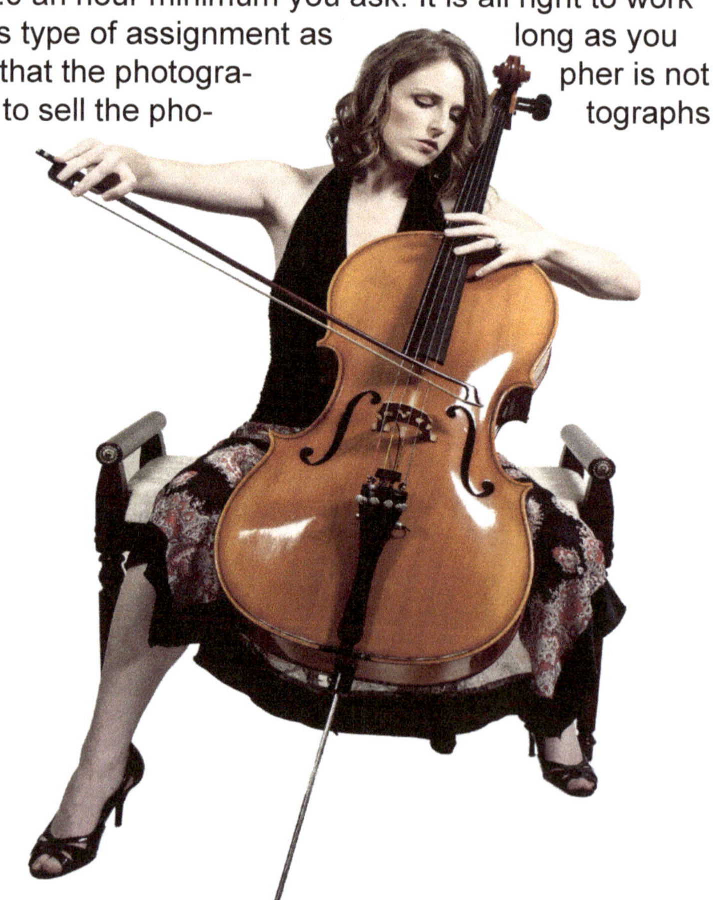

(do not sign any release without that stipulation). In this case, you should insist on payment in prints. A basic figuring point is two or three 8x10 black and white prints per back and white roll shot and one color 8x10 per color roll shot. By looking at the most professional price lists, this will average out at over $30/hour, but will actually cost the photographer much less as he is "donating" his time and only paying the processing fees.

No matter what the assignment, the model must be very careful to not over-price herself. To do so might mean losing a job. However, she must be equally careful not to under-price herself. This can lead to creating an "amateur image" in the mind of the employer and will certainly result in lost jobs because the casting person wants a "professional" and not "amateur." This recently happened in one case where the model turned down a job that would have provided excellent exposure but was a nonpaying job. By insisting on being treated like a professional, he later landed the company's television account. This was simply because the client said "print is OK for an amateur, but we never would have used an amateur on television."

Sometimes it hurts to say "no" but the model must look at tomorrow as well as today. She must always consider her career in making any decision, not just her immediate needs.

There are always exceptions to the rule. There are times when providing free work or free releases can be a good business and professional decision. This is a situation-based decision. If you are making a trade – your work for someone else's work – then it may be a good deal to do free work. Perhaps a photographer wants a special shot for his portfolio; doing a "free" shoot in exchange for a copy of the print, reprint rights, and maybe a few more shots, can provide valuable exposure for the model when the photographer pitches his work. It can also add a classic photo to your stock for your portfolio or composite.

Photographers appreciate this and often throw work to those who help them out. As much as we may want to think that it is our skill and talent that lands the job, more often than not it is our personal relationship and friendship that, if nothing else, opens the door to the casting office or lands the job that is cast without an open call.

If you have a photo in our portfolio and someone wants to use it in a special project, low or no fees can also be considered without breaking the professional pay rule. Look at what you can pull out of the project before making a final decision: will it provide you with a credit that you can use as a "tear sheet"; will it provide a professional credit that will help boost your career; will the work be credited and seen by people who are potential clients?

As an agent, I saw a lot of requests for free or discounted work cross my desk. Many I would not even consider. Frankly, some of those offers came from producers or photographers that I did not trust; people that I thought were not being honest with their project description or resources. Some I did not think had the potential for later income. As an agent, I only made 15% from the talent fees, so why should I spend the time contacting models and actors for projects that paid nothing today if I did not think that building a relationship in the future was worth the effort? Basic math still says that fifteen percent of nothing is ... well, nothing.

One of the key factors in considering the merit of a project was the backing behind the project. If a photographer was working on his own portfolio, then I had no problem helping if possible - I expected the photographer to help out the model with prints or significant discounts later. The cover of the first *Handbook* came from such an assignment.

The cover was originally a portfolio piece for the photographer, Les Benton. It turned out so well that we used it on the First Edition cover and it was a prominent piece in both models' portfolios. Every model who bought the book or casting director who received a free copy, saw

Les' work and the two girls right up front. It benefited all three with later assignments.

***Tip: These are all good reasons to step out of the "I only work for pay" box. Sometimes working for "barter" is not only acceptable it is a good idea.***

Think of it as an investment for the future. If the person behind the project is a small company trying to "get something going," helping is fine to do a trade. If it is a large company, they should pay. I once had a request for a dozen scantily-clad models for a Humble Pie music video. The Producer thought that just being in the video was enough of a thrill. So they wanted the girls at no cost I thought it was a joke. But the producer was serious. He was also serious when he said that these "free" models should be willing to appear topless.

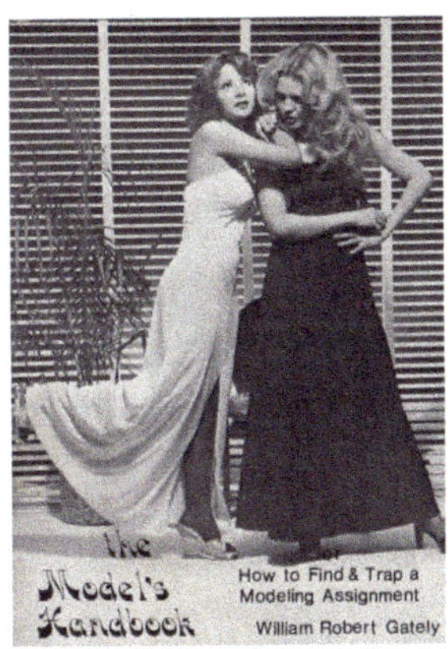


This is exactly the kind of scam an agent needs to be watching for in this industry. People are always wanting something for nothing.

Sometimes that is OK, but there was no "value received" here for the girl, not even promises of copies of the shoot.

In today's dominantly digital age, the up-front costs are not that much, excluding the cost of equipment. Work out something of reasonable value up front. It is difficult to base a price on the number of shots taken. Since there are no processing and printing costs, the photographer may take 100 shots where before he would stop at 36. In this case, you should ask for at least one 11x14 and a set number of 8x10 prints based on how long you work. If you need to buy a large USB drive or a portable hard drive to secure the photos, the cost is worthwhile.

Pricing professional work is more difficult. For television and film work, check with the local SAG or AFTRA office. They are the same union now, but some areas still have different rules for different work. Even if you are not a Union member, their rate structure is fair and will give you a starting point.

Local companies may not be able to afford union rates and, as you are not a member, you may go below the union fees, but always use their figures as a bargaining point. It may sound like a lot, but $15 an hour is only $120 for eight hours. Compared to a union rate of $627, that is dirt cheap. Union standards set the industry level for professional work and I would never recommend working for less than $100 a day - which is not much over minimum wage. Below minimum in some places where burger flippers make $15 an hour.

Print rates are even more difficult. For local work, $20-60/hr seems to be the going rate (except in L.A., Chicago, and New York). Start out at the lower end and give yourself raises slowly as you gain experience and a reputation.

Do not expect to make it rich all at once. You will need to build a good, steady clientele that has faith in your abilities before you can expect to ask for more. If you are unsure what rates are being charged in your area, call a local agency and ask what their beginning models are

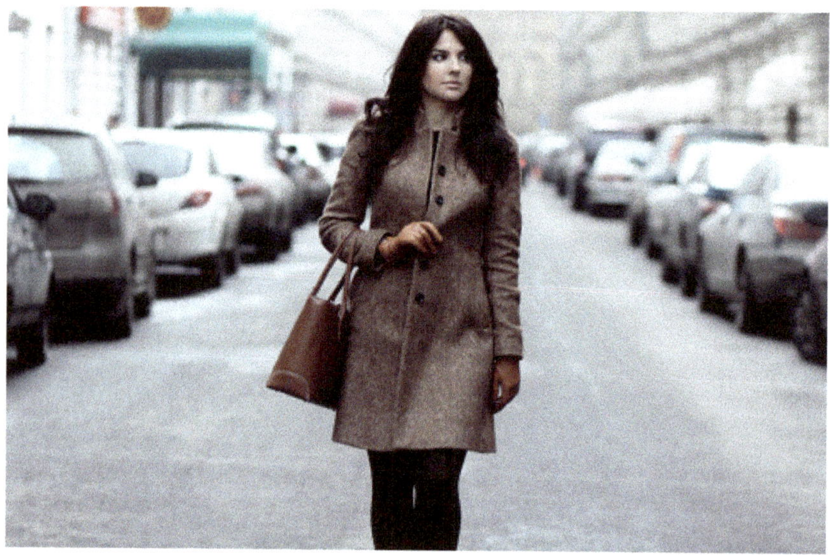

making. Then start $5-10 below that figure. In very large markets (over 1,000,000 populations) it may be best to find a good agent and let him/her handle the financial scene. This frees you to concentrate on the artistic and marketing aspects.

For national and large market ads, it is much more difficult to price a job. Catalogue modeling can run upwards of $100 per hour. Some print ads may pay $500 per session and include residuals, with a session lasting for 8-10 hours. In cases like these, until you have gained the experience and knowledge to properly price your worth, seek help in determining the proper pay rate.

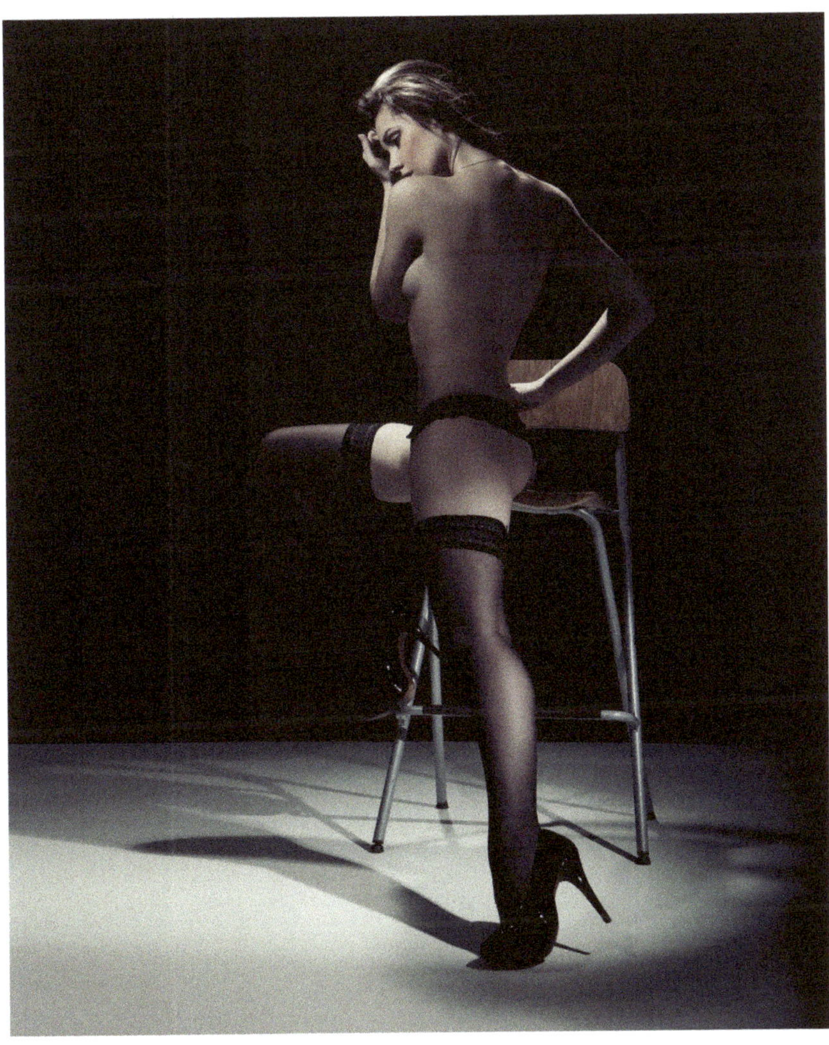

# 3 FINDING THE ASSIGNMENT

## ADVERTISING AGENCIES

Most modeling assignments come either directly or indirectly (through a talent agent or casting director) from an advertising agency. An ad agency spends a good deal of time looking for clients and then trying to talk them into spending money on advertising. Very often, these ads will use models and other talent. Since the ad agency can only make a good living by servicing several different companies, they are excellent places for the model to become known. It is a one-stop-shopping place to meet the casting representative of several companies that might use models.

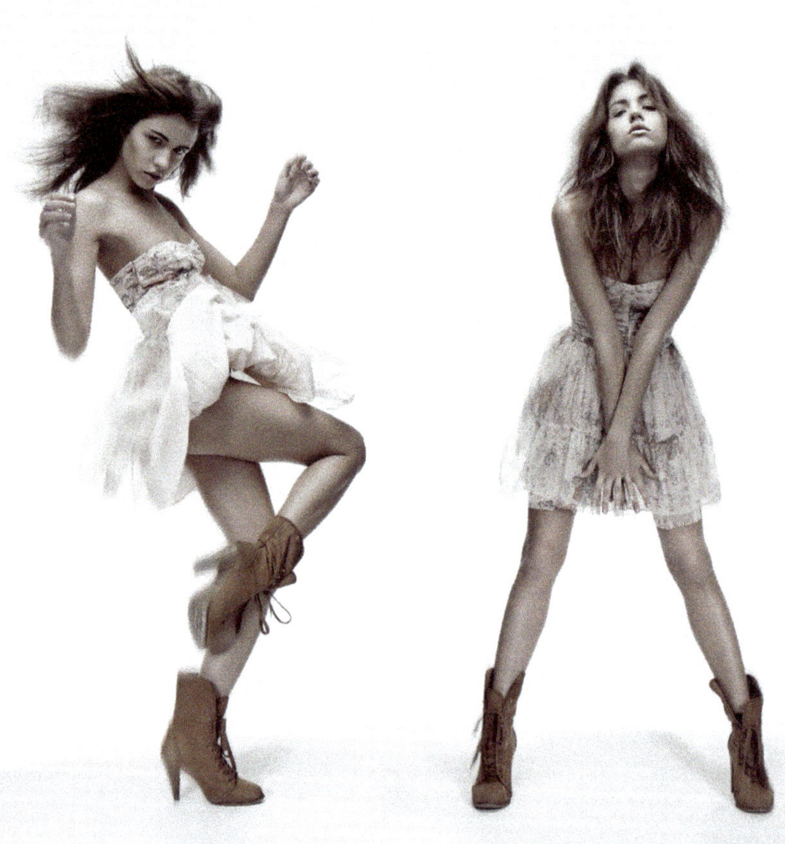

There are two things you can expect from an ad agency: the demand to see quality photographs at your interview (your portfolio) and the demand that you provide a photo or several photos (you composites) before you leave. Expect nothing else from them. Some will be polite, others decidedly not so. Most will not have any work for you then, but your goal is to have them keep you in mind should something come up. Some - a very few - might actually have something at that time. In any case, they will all want to see what you can do in the form of photographs.

Make your appointment with the Art Director, or Creative Director, if the company is large enough to have one. If not, ask to see the talent manager or owner. Even small agencies hire talent. Always go in person; do not rely on mail or phone interviews. It is too easy for a secretary to put you off over the telephone. If the person you need to see is not in, set an appointment then and there. Do not let some power hungry assistant put you off – this is your means of survival.

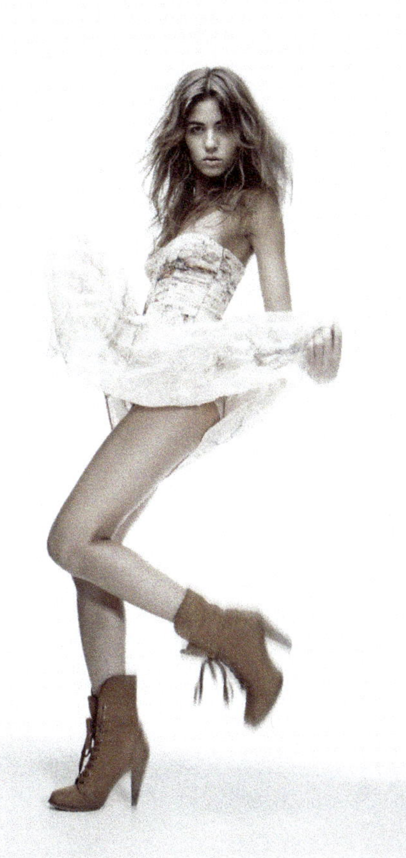

After you have met and talked to the casting supervisors, drop back in occasionally. If they are not in, leave a card or a composite or a new headshot. If they are in, just talk a few minutes; do not take a lot of their time, as they like to think that they are busy people.

The best time to visit advertising agencies is in the morning between 10:00 and 11:30 and afternoons between 1:30 and 3:30. That leaves time to go shopping and generally twiddle your thumbs. Take a good book on modeling, auditioning, or acting with you to help pass the time while the ad people are "out to lunch."

Be nice to these people as they will be one of your most valuable resources. They are the ones who have direct access to the big spending clients.

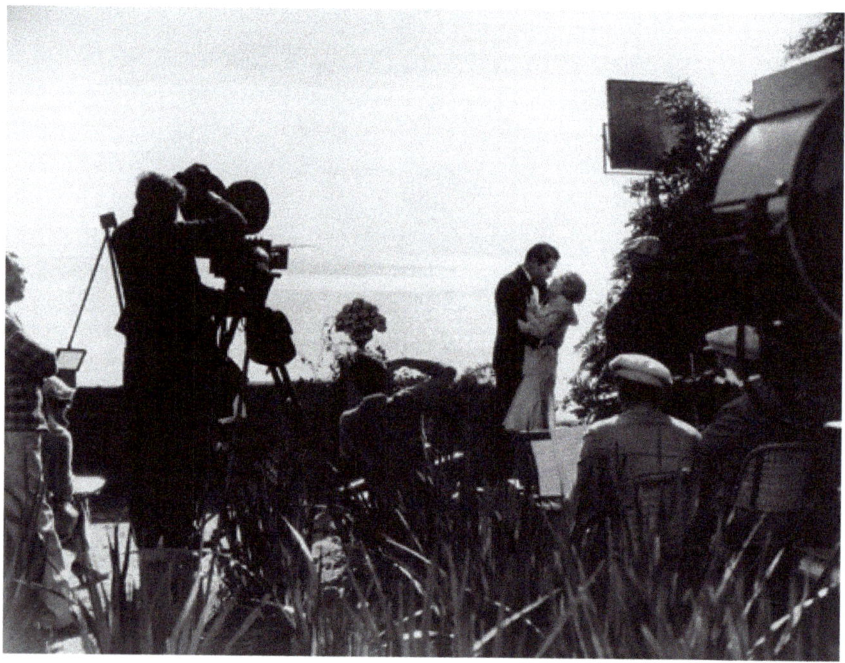

## VIDEO PRODUCERS

Occasionally, companies will script their own commercials or go directly to a video production company, bypassing the advertising agency. If you have an acting background and/or good vocal training, then it will be worth your time to seek out and meet the video producers. Actually, it is not a bad idea even without training since video producers often cast for non-speaking parts. The producers usually work with locally produced commercials. National commercials are more often produced through ad agencies on the national releases or regional spots. While the local work is not as lucrative as national spots, every little bit helps.

Video producers often ask for a video ("reel") of something you have done. If you do not have a tape, try to get one. Sometimes video production companies may tape you when you go in for an interview, but this is not available to you and an audition for a specific company is seldom of valuable to another producer. So you need to work on a generic "reel" that will have some sample commercial pitches, a monologue, and any video "cut sheets" from online work you have done. Keep it under five minutes. Fewer than three is better. Just about one minute is best.

***Tip: Casting people are busy. Keep your audition material short and to the point. Make a new tape specifically for each audition.***

Local producers will ask you to leave a composite or a headshot. Video producers are usually less sophisticated in their photo requests than print casting agents, so a headshot may do, but I have sat in on many a post-audition session where headshots were tossed or forgotten where composites, or composites attached to a headshot, end up in the call-back pile for no better rea-

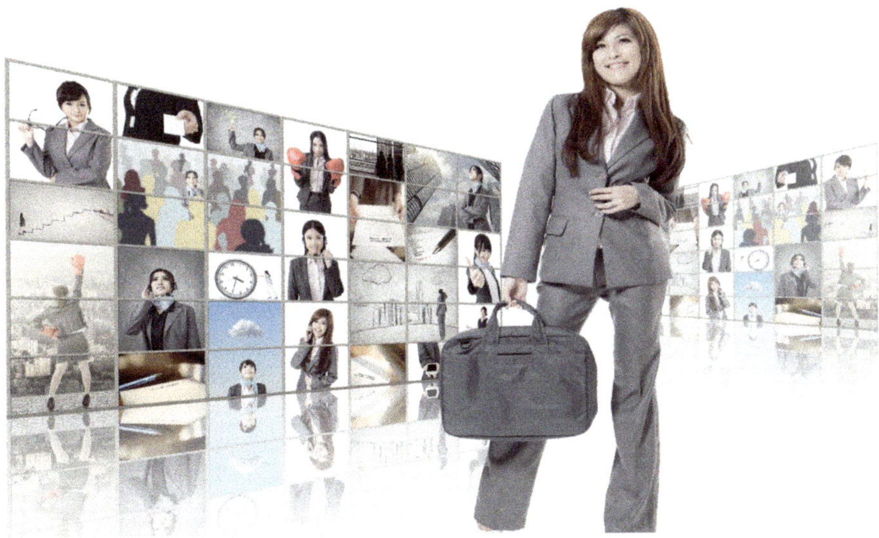

son than that the single headshot does not look quite like what they are casting but something on the composite is exactly what they want.

A reel is also important if a client is out of town or not available for the audition. You may be asked to leave several copies. Do so. That is why you have them. They may also request additional composites or headshots. If you land a job with them, immediately or later, the minor expense is well worth the additional cost of multiple copies.

Reels are important tool and, these days, not that expensive to produce. Make contacts, network; decent video equipment is not that expensive and someone will have what you need - even college students - to produce a high quality video. If you are careful with lighting and audio, you can easily produce a professional looking video for little or no money. Do not - repeat NOT - try to use a cell phone to produce your tape. Frankly, you are not likely to impress anyone in a positive way. Do it right or don't do it. Right, however, does not always mean expensive.

Here are the basics for making a competitive reel:

1. Good lighting and audio are at the top of the list - take your time and make it right. You need to look and sound good on a laptop, tablet, or even a cell phone.

2. Use a solid color background, something that is not shinny or distracting.

3. Never slate - titling each segment - unless asked.

4. Keep a script in your hand - it suggests that you are flexible and can be coached. Though you may have memorized the script, it is a good psychological ploy. Do this at live auditions, too. It eases the worry that you will need a line prompt.

5. Stay in the center of the frame. DO NOT move the camera or get artsy. It is OK if you step into the

scene (that shows you can hit a mark) but keep the camera locked firmly on the tripod. You want nothing to distract the viewer. Sitting or standing should be dictated by the material, not whim.

6. Follow all instructions. Exactly. Precisely. With no embellishment. Mistakes in file names, lighting, format, whatever, can lead to having your audition ignored.

7. Don't use a cell phone. Use a real - if inexpensive - camera.

8. Shoot each scene individually. Edit later, but avoid on-screen transitions. The nice thing about tape is that you can take the time to do it right and re-do the scene as often as it takes to deliver your best performance for the interview.

9. Select material that is succinct and shows your talent. Rely on clips, short snapshots of your work (runway, a series of still shots, etc.). Remember, you are trying to show them how you look and sound. Only select high quality samples from the DVD, CD, or downloads the producer gives you.

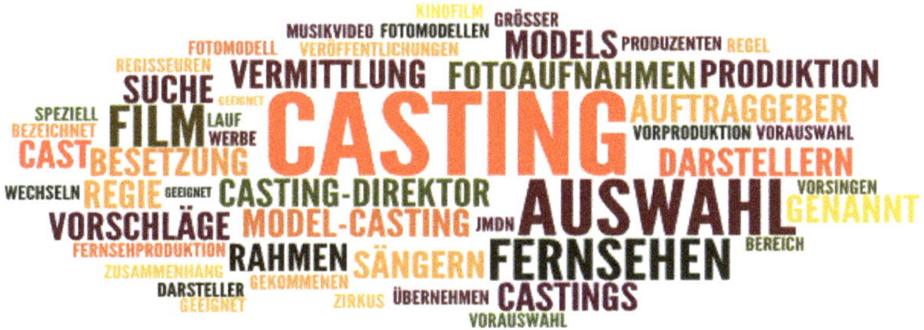


## Casting Agents

Casting agents are strange creatures. I ran into my first one in 1969. I didn't understand what she wanted then and I still find it difficult to develop a clear picture of the way a casting agent's mind works. I have lost count of how often a character description would call for tall and dark and the agent would cast short and fat. It is just as bad in modeling. Sometimes the casting agent has a clear image and casts for the look, regardless of talent. Sometimes what they image they want is vague. Those are the ones that the talent agent can work with the best. If they are flexible, talent agents have more room to work in choosing talent to submit for a part; they can work with ability in addition to looks in putting together an agency proposal.

The absolute worse casting agents are those that are "sleeping" with a select group of agents. When a part comes up, the casting agent only calls one or two talent agents, a handful of friends, and pulls a sprinkling of headshots from their files. That tends to limit the talent pool, something that hurts both the producer and the market, but we see it much too often in the smaller markets. This is a very tough business and way too often people work too hard to keep others out even if they are excluding the best talent for a project.

This is especially true and troubling outside the Los Angeles and New York markets. A talent community that is too narrow will not attract print or film producers from the production Meccas of LA, NY, Chicago, and Detroit. That means less work all the way around. A small talent pool is quickly worked out and, if there is not enough variety in that pool, the producers tend to shoot elsewhere.

Unfortunately, this produces a "Catch 22" in marketing yourself. Limiting a casting call to only a few select agencies is bad for everyone, even the chosen agencies. It is a practice that the Screen Actors Guild and the American Federation of Television and Radio Artists has aggressively fought (with limited results) ever since before I joined the industry – almost a half century.

The best way to force unethical casting agents – and make no mistake, this form of casting nepotism is highly unethical – is for the talent to boycott the casting agents. If they cannot attract talent to a casting call, then produc-

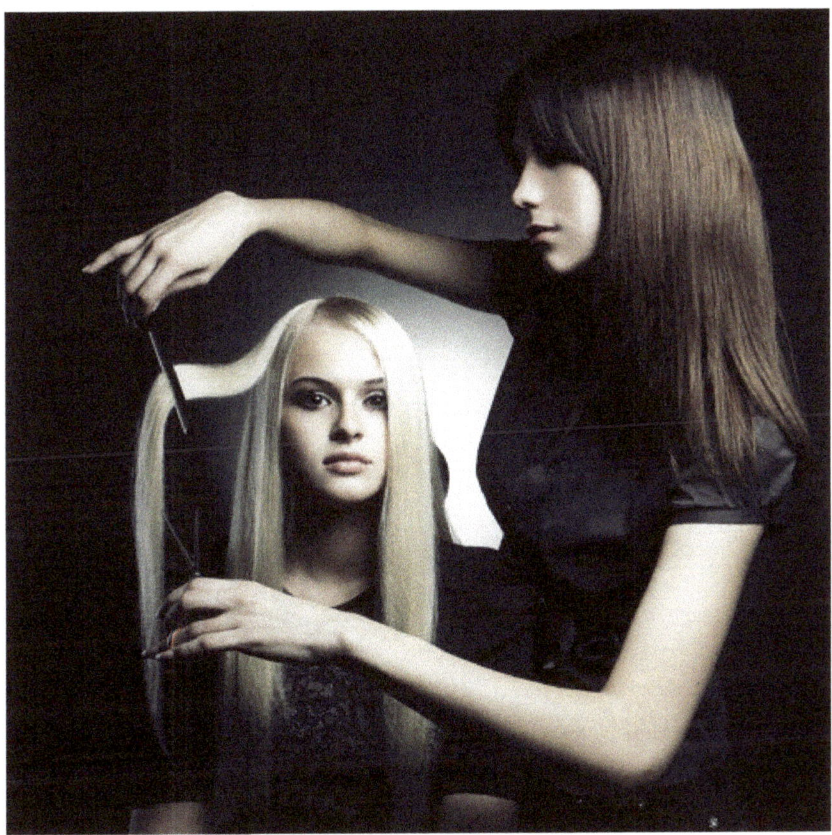

ers will use other, more inclusive agents, and the unprofessional “good buddy” agent will disappear.

Do not expect a boycott to work. The best one can hope for is a ban by the union, preventing union talent from attending castings held by closed casting agents, and that is an unlikely action in most cases. Expecting models and actors to ban together for the benefit of the talent community is also a dream. If their agent is one of the chosen few, it is the rare actor or model who will welcome competition from other agents. Let's face it: there is enough competition inside an agency to get on that call sheet much less opening up to others. However, there is something to be said for a larger number of small agencies where the number of people of a certain type is lower. Everyone has a better chance of making the call if two people from eight agencies go rather than three people from four.

By nature, actors and models are independent. They are all fighting for the same small slice of a relatively small pie. On a large scale, cooperation, sharing of leads, boycotting casting agents who use unethical practices is not something that will occur in nature; though it may happen in isolated cases, it is not a reasonable industry-wide expectation.

This is a difficult call and one too often played out every day across the country. Cities like Miami, Phoenix, Dallas, Cincinnati, and Atlanta, which should be large enough to have outgrown the small town influence attitudes, are just as bad as the smaller markets like Tucson, San Antonio, Orlando, San Francisco, and the like. It is only seldom that legitimate casting calls are publicized outside of professional Internet forums.

So the novice or the person just out of the loop is uninformed. The scenario of "what if they gave a casting call and nobody come" is only conceivable if nobody knows about the call!

What is a professional to do? As much as I hate to say it, they must play the game or accept that they will never work for a specific casting agent. That is a hard decision for a model who has an agent who is honest, hardworking, and moderately easy to get along with and the main (or only) casting agent in town is a long-time friend with your agent's competition. Somehow your agent never receives a call when a casting session is booked.

***Tip: Disregard how obnoxious any individual casting agent may be. Ultimately, they are the gate keeper of your career.***

The way around that is a personal visit casting agent. If you are the right type and you are good, your agent may get a call requesting you specifically. Personal contact is the only way to by-pass industry bias.

Get to know the casting agents in your area. Be friends. Be professional. You will get calls even if your agency does not. Keep a good agent. Work.

Best of all worlds.

Look at what is going on in your community. Talk to other actors/models about the casting agents. Identify the unethical, petty, or call-only-my-friends casting agent. Then make a choice: either write them off as a lost cause, or play around their game.

With all casting agents, the personal contact is vital. They need to know you and know what you can do if you have any hope of being singled out and called for a special casting call. The flaky ones are even more important to get to know: they often thrive on the ego boost from talent paying them special attention.

Casting agents, more than any other potential employer, need to know what special talents you have and abilities or services you offer. Can you ride a horse or a motorcycle? If so, make sure they know it and that they know what equipment or livestock you have available.

Can you juggle, walk on stilts, dance on a tightrope? Do you sing or play an instrument?

These are skills that may not be on your resume, especially if they are not well developed skills but hobbies, but they need to be on the material you have left with the casting agents. A good casting agent has a cross-referenced file on all the talent in the area so they can find special needs quickly and efficiently. The agent needs to know what you can do, and reminding them of that special talent occasionally is not out of line.

Always be nice and polite to casting agents. That does not mean sleep with them (which can kill your career faster than you might think), just be nice and professional. If the casting director offers workshops, it would not be a bad idea to take a few.

Never, never, never badmouth a casting agent for any reason. It will get back to them. Guaranteed. The predatory nature of the industry insures that someone will carry tales to generate an advantage.

***Tip: Casting Directors work for a media producer. A Casting Agent is an independent individual or company who works for hire on many different projects.***

The exception to the rule: if a casting agent has demonstrated verifiable unethical conduct, then people need to know so action can be taken. The key here is unethical. If you have proof, take it to authorities or union, not the grapevine.

SAG/AFTRA secretaries are human and their skills, interests, level of involvement, and capabilities differ from person to person. The union, however, has a vested interest in keeping the industry policed. Even people causing problems for non-union members are of concern since they may contract union members, also. Take the time to inform the local union of any ethics concerns. They may not take it anywhere, or they may not take it anywhere fast, but they do deserve to be consulted.

If the infraction involves money or demands for sexual favors, the police may be interested. The days when casting couches and back room deals were common are gone. They still exist – more than many of us would wish to acknowledge – but they are now more the exception than the rule because of the legal consequences with sexual harassment. Do not be afraid to "be a whistle-blower."

***TIP: A casting agent never requires a fee from talent.***

Casting Agents do require good composites and a constant update to your files. Every time you work, no matter who cast the part or cast the photo shoot or scheduled the fashion show, it 87is a credit. Update your credits with casting agents as often as possible. In fact, if you are working often and not cast by a specific agent, rub their nose in it a little. If you are a hot talent and not being presented to an agent's clients, they are losing money, the client is not seeing the best choices, and the casting agent stands the chance to lose money and clients if their talent selections are not perfect for the job.

Remember, Casting Agents - the same as salaried Casting Directors - are hired to find the best talent for an assignment. If they are ignoring a good talent for personal reasons, they are hurting themselves in the long run. Keeping an agent well-informed about your rising career is the best way to end up on that agent's "also call" list even if they are avoiding your talent agent.

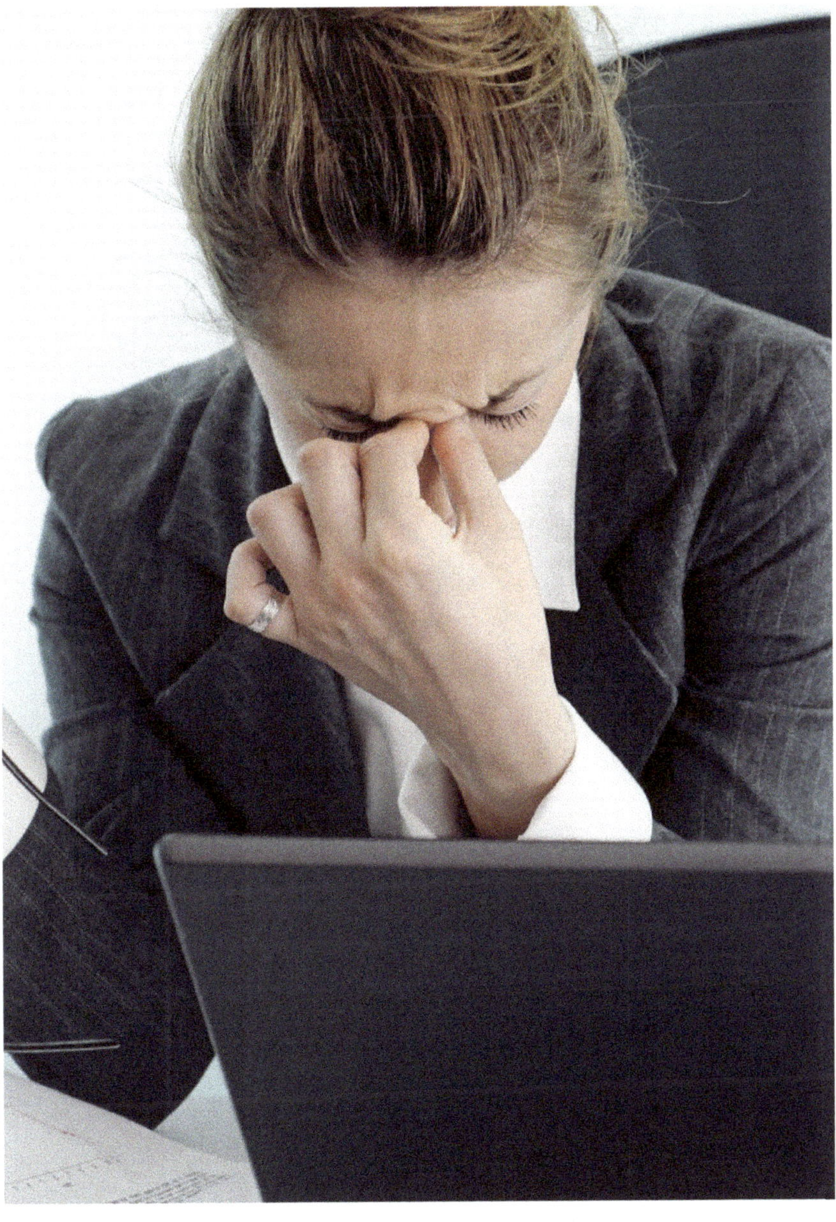

Rarely, but occasionally, a talent who is loyal to their agent, treats biased casting agents with respect, and maintains a professional attitude, can help change the nature of a community's attitude and approach to casting calls.

## WHAT CASTING DIRECTORS WANT

One of the many eye-opening revelations I had early in the industry is that casting agents, directors, and producers often do not have a clue what they want for their productions. They may think they do, they may say the do, but often enough, they have no clue. That is reasonable. If the client has an image in their head, the only way to share that image with a casting director is with a photo, someone who looks like what they are seeing in their mind's eye that the director tries to match.

One of the first movies where I was active in pitching talent was a film called "KidCo." The film was shot in Tucson, 140 miles away from Phoenix, where my agency was located. After several trips for casting calls, we had a couple of children cast but not much else. The casting agent called and complained

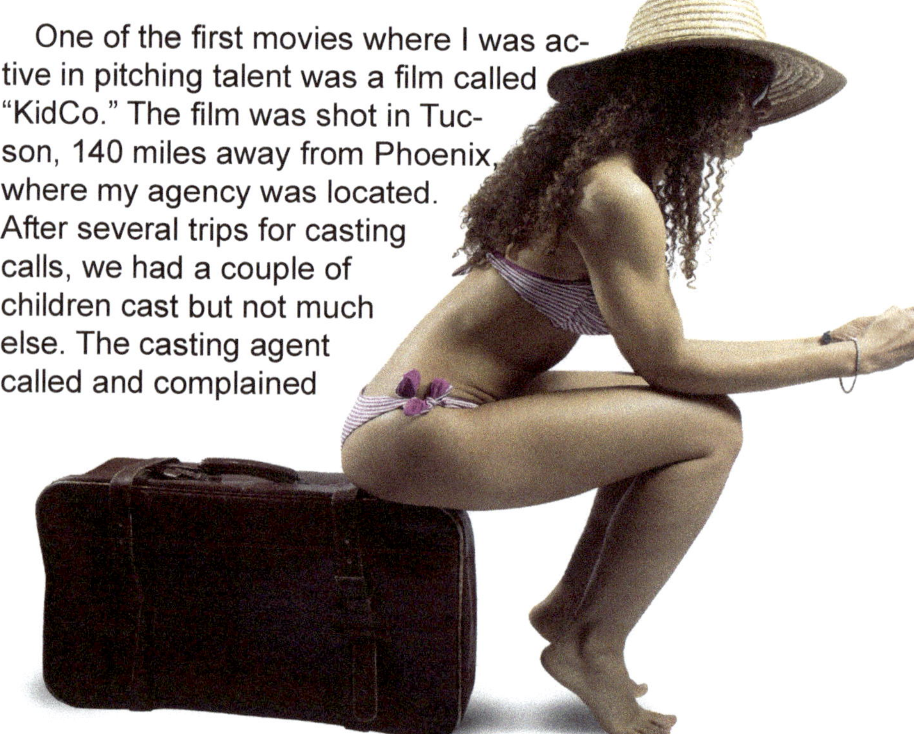

that they could not find an "authentic" looking actor for the part of a policeman in the film. This was not a major role, but in a film, everything must "fit" or the production will not look or feel the way the producer expects.

I had, at that time, two or three policemen from the Phoenix Police Department signed up. I pitched them, but the casting director said they did not look like policemen. Go figure. So I pitched a female police officer, an excellent actress, and, coincidentally, the mother of two of the children already cast in the film.

No, no, I was told. No women. This part was for a cop, a big burly cop, tough and imposing and forget that she could provide her own uniform. Certainly, this mother of two, petite, blond, and very pretty, did not fit that description. But, as I said, she was an excellent actress and I was not to be daunted, especially since it left the agency without representation in the special casting session they were holding for that part.

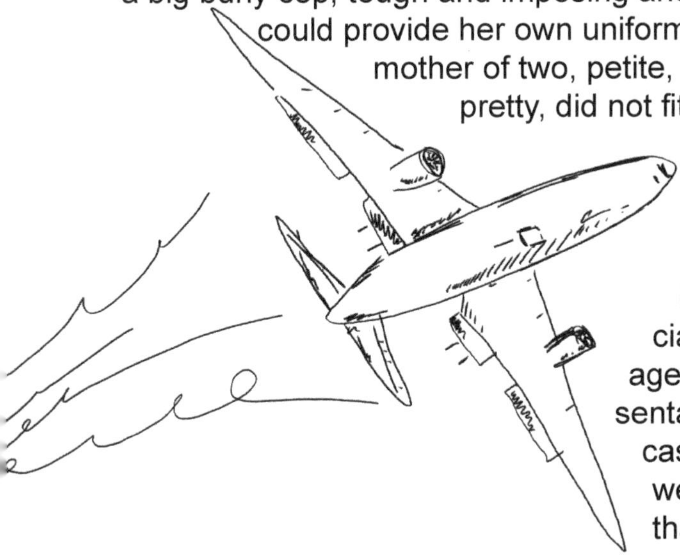

There may be something to the shark image that talent agents have, but most talent agents I know do not try to bite their clients. (That's most, not all.) Instead, they are aggressive in putting their talent before the casting agent; especially legitimate agents who are limited to a small percentage of the talent's fee. Union work, which includes most feature films and national television commercials, is limited to 10% and, like 15%, 10% of nothing is nothing.

This young lady had a fitting scheduled for her children on the same day as the casting session. I told her to don her uniform, take the kids in early and mumble something about a tight work schedule. Oh, and make sure she stopped by the casting office at the hotel to ask directions to the fitting room.

OK, you guessed the ending. She landed several days on the film as the police officer in question. She was completely opposite of the part's description, but she shoved the casting director's nose in the fact that she looked like a cop and could act like a cop.

This makes it very difficult when a casting agent calls and wants a 5'8" blond for a part and you know that a 5'5" redhead is perfect. If you send the redhead, the casting agent's client may decided she is perfect; but more likely, the agent will throw a fit that you were wasting her time with the wrong "type." And yet time and again, the "wrong type" person was cast for the role. This would happen because I would get a call for the blonds - send three - and, oh, that little redhead? Send her too.

Why? Because they had met the redhead and knew what she could do. Casting agents are not stupid (usually). They know that their client wants that best person for the part. Sometimes it doesn't hurt to invite someone who is not quite right but who is quite good. The contrast often is what swings the decision.

I am firmly convinced that it is the rare casting agent who can imagine an actor in a part. *You* have to become the part to be noticed. *You* have to take the imagination out of the part. That is the main reason that composites work better than headshots in most casting sessions for films. The composites may just have a picture of you in a character that is similar to what the producers are trying to cast. They do not have to think about the part. If you can act, your photo shows that you can look the part. You have just made the casting agent's job easy – they don't have to think.

So when do you use a composite and when do you use a headshot and when do you leave a reel on CD or DVD? This is not always an easy call. Certainly, when you are uncomfortable in a casting, drop a headshot, cut your costs, and look for the next assignment.

But, when in doubt, leave a composite and hope. You can never wear a thin skin, though. Most actors/models should feel lucky if they land one out of one hundred casting calls. The odds, however, are much, much better when you have made contact with the casting agent on a previous session or in their offices and they have invited you for the current session. There is no substitute for personal contact.

***Tip: Casting agents are your bread and butter. Treat them well. Most are pretty decent people.***

## TALENT AGENTS

Contrary to popular belief, talent agents are not in business to find work for actors and models. Talent agencies are in business to find work for the agency. That means that the job of finding work for you is up to you. You need to visit casting directors, art directors, photographers, video producers, film producers, and catalog manufactures to insure that when a casting call goes into your agent that your name ends up on a call list. It is even better if they request you by name.

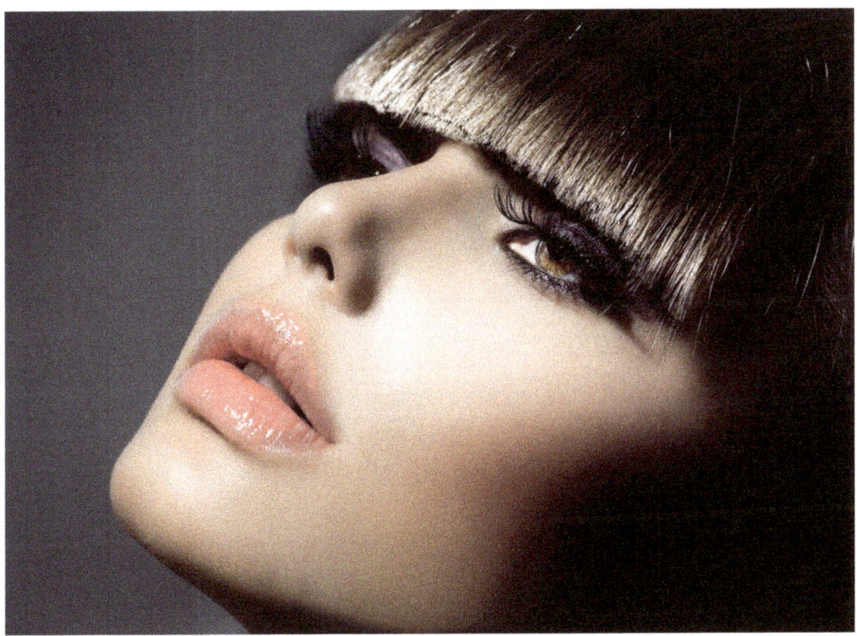

Essentially, where an agent is useful in finding work is mainly with casting sessions from out of the area, usually New York or Los Angles film or advertising calls. These are the people you are less likely to reach on your own and who might come into town and contact agents directly for a casting call. Many larger companies from the major media hubs will hire a casting agent local to their area, someone they have worked with and trust. That agent will reach out to local talent agents and arrange castings. There is no sure-fire way of reaching them outside the talent agency pipeline.

Even so, you are not guaranteed a spot on the call even if your agent has the opportunity to pitch you. Casting agents tell the talent agent what they want based on sex, age, height, hair color, special talents, how they need to match up with other cast members who may be related in the script, and so on. If you do not fit those basic characteristics, then it is unlikely you will end up on the call sheet.

A talent agent is often also given a quota on the casting call, most commonly three people per part in the first round. If the part is not cast right off, there are occasionally additional calls, but assume that any call is limited to three people per role. If the part calls for a blond, 5'5" to 5'7", proportional weight, with some acting skills, it is possible that an agency may represent several dozen potential candidates. Who will receive the call? Favorites? Sometimes. The most skilled? Likely choice. The person with the most credits? Put that at the top of the list. The one who shows the most interest, professionalism, persistence (without being a pest) and willingness to expend effort on their own behave? Almost certainly.

Why? Because the motivated model or actress is most likely to bring business into the agency over and above the agency's efforts. In the long run, that means more money for the agency. Sometimes favorites are "favorites" precisely because of their professional effort and not for any special services performed for or personal relationship with the agent. Those favorites are hard to beat out and should not be looked on too poorly.

An agent who relies on personal reasons for casting will eventually pay for those choices. An agent who sends the best talent with the most invested in her career, thrives.

Now that you know how to feed and care for a talent agent, what breed will produce the best results?

The first clue is in where the agency receives the most of their income. Is it commissions from promoting and managing models? Or is the talent agent interested in running a school or a photo factory? Note what they offer in the way of training and photography help, but be very weary if they suggest classes that they offer even if they are not required, especially if they make the suggestion strongly, unless the classes are free or not very expensive (make-up training is always helpful if done right).

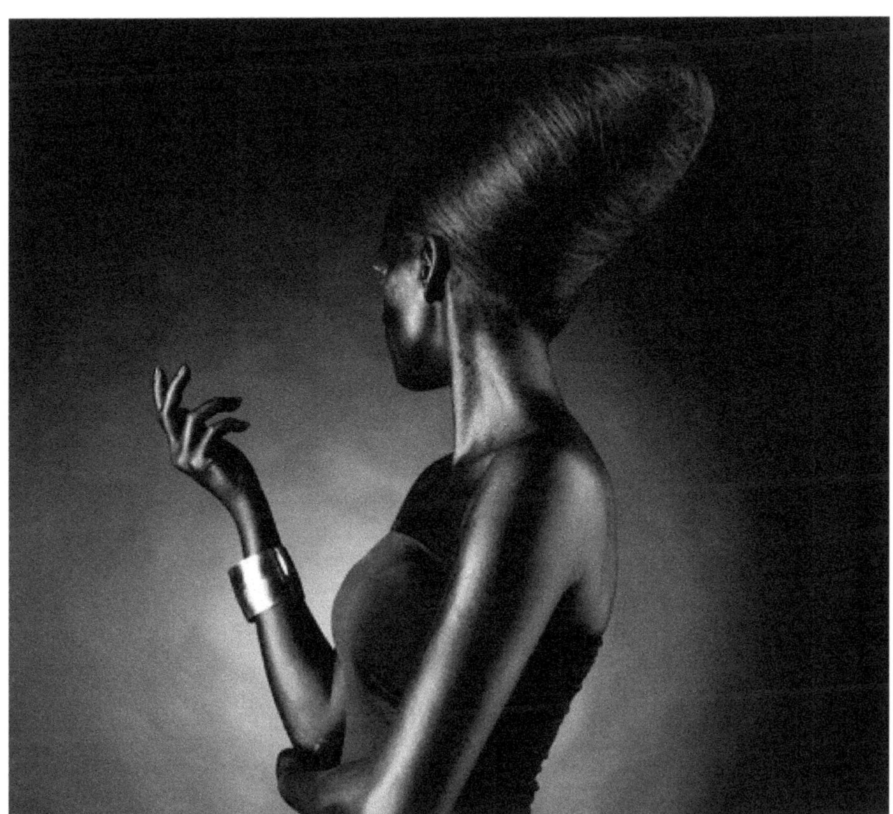

You need to be very honest with yourself. Evaluate your looks, your talent, and your experience level. You may need lessons. But you might find everything you need at the local community college for a fraction of the cost; without ties to a specific agent. Try a Community College for classes that cover a broader range of topics, and classes that may give you college credit. But be brutal. Improving yourself may take time and money; still, there is no need to throw it away on over-priced workshops.

Sometimes talent agents will offer workshops by actors, models, voice-over talent, or casting agents that can be very helpful and informative, especially if they are taught by working talent. They can also be good networking opportunities. Take advantage of these, but run if you are pushed toward courses that may cost you thousands of dollars.

Another exception that is prevalent today more so that in the years past, is the finishing course. If this is offered (not required!), then it may be worth your time and money. Perception is reality in this industry and knowing how to walk and talk and sit and get in and out of a car without exposing too much can have its value. There really is a difference in how you walk, sit, stand up, and get out of a

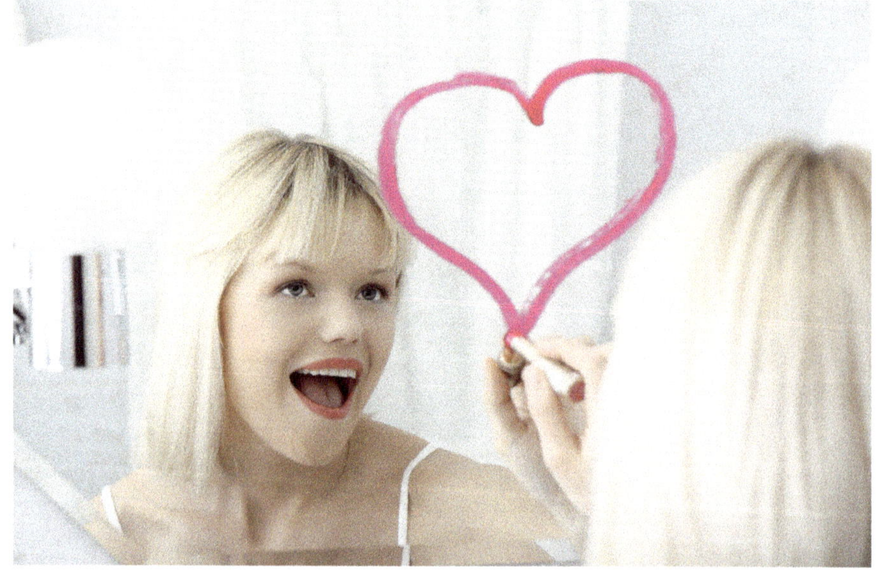

car that can mark you as a professional or someone who missed "finishing classes" as a child.

These are important skills for auditions and when visiting advertising agencies. Photographers and film producers will notice the difference, but they are less likely to be aware of the missing social graces, often lacking them themselves. Still, class is noted, even if it is only a veneer, and can help land a high-paying project.

Avoid agencies that are little more than photo factories. There were several in the early eighties – they seemed to pop up every other week – and they still surface occasionally today. These agents sign anyone who walks in the door as long as they will spend a few hundred dollars buying some assembly-line headshots of marginal quality, no creativity, and no value. The talent may have some use for the photos, but the agents do little more than paste them on the wall to sucker in new buyers (talent) and throw the rest in boxes for later disposal. These agents seldom last more than a year.

Most agencies will screen photographers and suggest you work with one off a list of a half dozen or so the agency believes will do the type of work they want at a reasonable price. Do not work with an agency that limits your choices to their approved list. If an agent is receiving a kickback from the photographer, it is not likely a healthy relationship for the model no matter how much it excites the agent. Rather than an approved list, my agency kept a list of photographers who were sub-standard in quality or professionalism.

Look closely at "promotional fees," "signing fees," or other charges that do not have a tangible return. Most states require a talent agent to obtain a license, often the same as an employment agency, and up-front fees are regulated or illegal for licensed agents.

The agent should also have a license from the state in which they are operating, not another state. Avoid agencies requiring fee-based monthly "updates" or who specialize in "out of state" modeling, which more often than not requires a little more labor than just posing. It is easy for a young talent to be intimidated into doing things she would not do otherwise if she is alone, away from home, and frightened. Or drugged.

Usually an agency will require an exclusive contract that gives the agent a 10%-20% commission on all work that the model does, regardless who finds the work. If it is a good agency, this is well worth the price as they can often land you interviews that you could not find on your own. They may also charge an extra fee to the producer. This is sometimes acceptable if it does not dramatically impact the rate paid the model for their work.

***Tip: Your agent only makes 10-15% of what you make. Don't expect them to do 85-90% of the work.***

A good agent acts as a phone service, handles contract negotiations, seeks out opportunities for the agency's talent, and generally relieves the talent of worry about the business side of the industry. If a company is slow in paying, the agency acts as a bill collector. This insulates the talent from the messier side of the business and can help the talent keep a good reputation in the industry even if producers think the agent is a snake.

A good agent will also help weed out the snakes in the producer ranks. Over time, an agent learns to identify scam artists, dreamers, porno purveyors, and general sleaze bags. Some will get through, but you are usually safer with an agent looking out for your interests.

When dealing with national accounts, assuming you can land one on your own, an agent is essential. Union and talent contracts are a legal nightmare and most agents understand that taking good care of talent is more profitable in the long run than letting the talent hang out on a limb alone.

Economically, the model will generally have to book over $3,000.00 a month to provide the basic services an agent offers for free without factoring in any legal costs or contract negotiations, even allowing for a full 15% of the income allocated to phone and promotional services. A good agent is a bargain.

One other point about agents: even when the talent finds the job on their own, the agent should handle the contract. This separates the talent from the negotiations and any unpleasantness in the negotiation or collection process. It is better to have a client angry with an agent than with the talent. Agencies are necessary to producers and a good agent will represent talent that the producer may want to use at a later date. There is mutual dependency that exists between the two businesses that does not exist between a producer and an individual. Use that to your advantage.

When a model contracts with an agent, it is usually an exclusive contract, as mentioned above. This means that the talent has a contractual obligation to run all work through the agent in addition to a moral or business reason. All commissions should be paid on every assignment. That is called having integrity.

That means that even if you find the work, negotiate the contract, perform the assignment, and collect the fee, the agent should still be paid. This might surprise

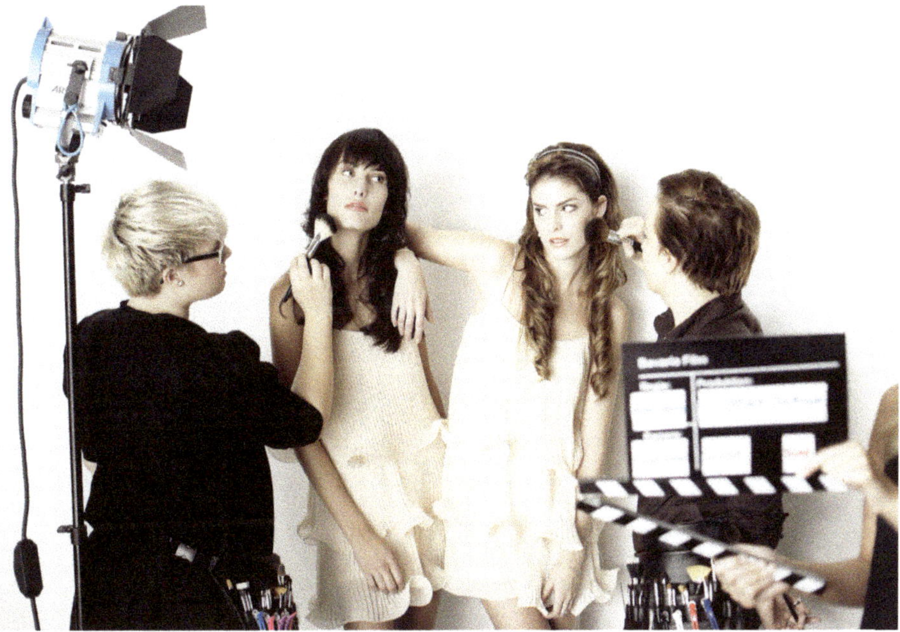

the agent, who is probably not used to dealing with honest people, but it will certainly insure his best efforts on your behalf. Your best bet is still to run as much directly through the agency as possible. This is for your protection and reputation, your professional image, and peace of mind. Just make sure you have an honest agent.

## TALENT MANAGERS

There is a difference between talent agents and talent managers. An agent's sole job and responsibility is to find work for talent in his/her agency. It doesn't matter which talent, as long as a person cast is from that agency. They are concerned, primarily, with finding work for talent, nothing more.

They are not concerned, nor do they spend much time, thinking about the talent's career. If you want guidance, if you want somebody to help you decide which assignments are good for you, for your career, and not just somebody who will sign you up on any job that comes along, then you need a manager not an agent. Or best yet, one of each.

While a talent manager may work to find jobs for you, while they may use their contacts in the industry to bring you to the attention of a variety of potential clients, their primary job is to guide you in your career development. They need to be critical of you, what you look like, how you act, how you dress, how your make-up looks, how you wear your hair, and which assignments you'll actually take. That means that a talent manager may turn down work for you. If the job or the assignment is something that may damage your career, and they'll tell you to walk away from it.

Also managers will help you, well, manage your life. He will take your money and assist you in investing it, saving it if you're making enough – even unknown international fashion models working overseas can make as much as $100,000 a year – put you on allowance so that when the assignments aren't stacking up you still have some money to live on. In essence, the manager's job is to guide you on your career as a model, as an actor/actress/ musician, and to assist you in achieving long-term success and sustainable in the industry.

What you can expect from an agent is someone who is out there looking for jobs which you may – or may not – be suitable for and which you may – or may not – be presented as part of a talent proposal.

What you might expect from a manager is to look at all the work the agent brings, sort through it, tell you which ones to take which ones to pass, and work on creating opportunities for you that are unique to you. A manager might try to get you into your own web show, or into branching out into other areas such as music or theater.

An agent finds you work, but a manager works to develop your career. A manager may very often be somebody who frustrates you and makes you angry because a good manager is not going to always give you what you want but will give you what you need. And yes, you might end up calling them mother.

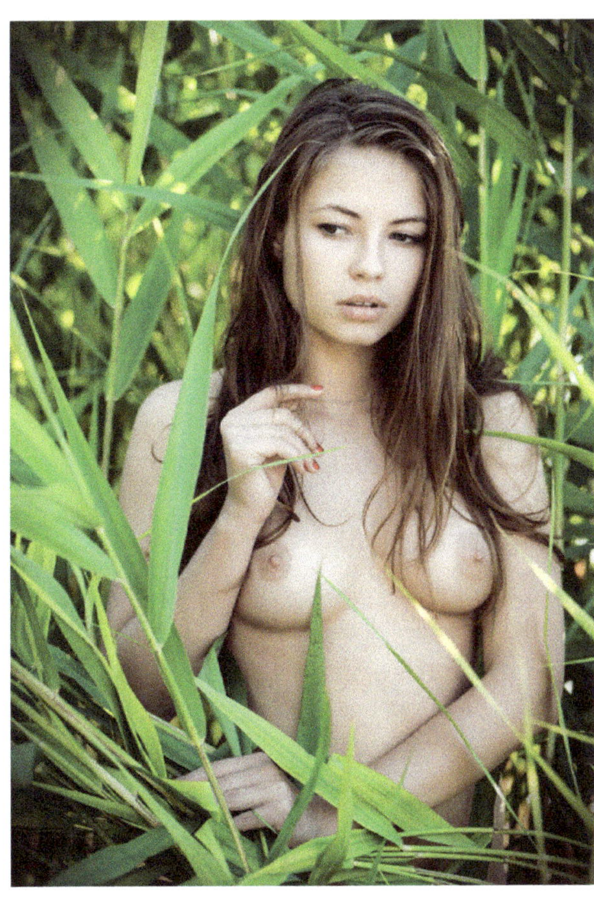

As a rule, managers are

much harder to secure than agents. Manages spend a lot more of their time working with you and you alone. They may only have two or three other clients as opposed to hundreds. They often advance their own money to help you get your career started.

Quite often models who have established themselves enough that clients come looking for them will replace the agents with the manager because at that point they need more help in managing their career than finding new work. Managers will say: "NO, don't take that job, it is bad for your career" and pass on their commission.

Which is right for you? If you're new in the industry, you might be better served with a manager than an agent. Because a manager is more likely to help you avoid mistakes that an agent be more than happy to push you into. However, it is hard to justify a manager at a time in your career when more jobs trumps better jobs. It is not an easy choice, but in most cases as a novice, you will not attract the attention of a manager.

## OTHER LEADS

Watch the newspapers and their online editions (specifically *Backstage* and *Variety*), Sunday magazines, and television commercials produced locally. These ads will direct you to advertising-minded companies who have hired talent in the recent past. Phone the company and locate the in-house ad manager or discover the name of their ad agency. This will tell you who to talk to about their next assignment.

Keep an eye on your LinkedIn Groups. You *do* have a LinkedIn account, right? And you *are* online regularly looking for announcements in the various actors' groups like Actor's Network, Independent Film and Producers, Acting, Modeling & Entertainment Socialites, Fashion Modeling Industry, Fashion Modeling Community, and several hundred more. Besides some excellent articles, there are casting notices posted.

You need to be pro-active in your look for work. It takes a lot of years and a lot of assignments before people come looking for you. Before that happens, you need to aggressively market yourself (aggressively, not obnoxiously) by sending your material to any - and every - assignment you can find that you think fits your look and talent. Have a thick skin as many "Nos" will follow.

Most people do not respond, some just say no, some are jerks... but it only takes one yes to begin building your portfolio of completed assignments. The bigger the portfolio is, the better chance you have of coming to the attention of the big money people.

Photographers and photographers' associations are also good sources for leads. Sometimes models' associations might work, but these organizations are seldom effective and are rife with in-fighting and politics. Private modeling schools will usually only work with their graduates, but they may have a bulletin board you can look at occasionally.

By keeping your eyes and ears open, you can locate many good contacts and references (like the events coordinator at the local department store) which will be of value to your career.

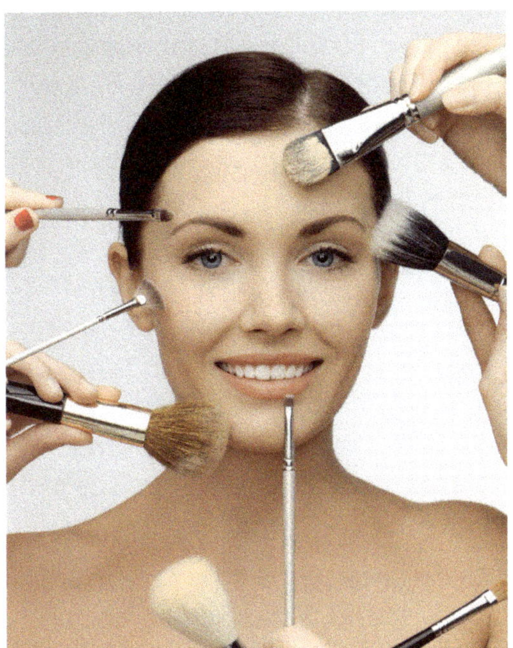

There are other associations for public relations professionals, videographers, and art directors. See if they are active in your city, obtain a mailing list, and send postcards and attend a few meetings.

Are you seeing a pattern?

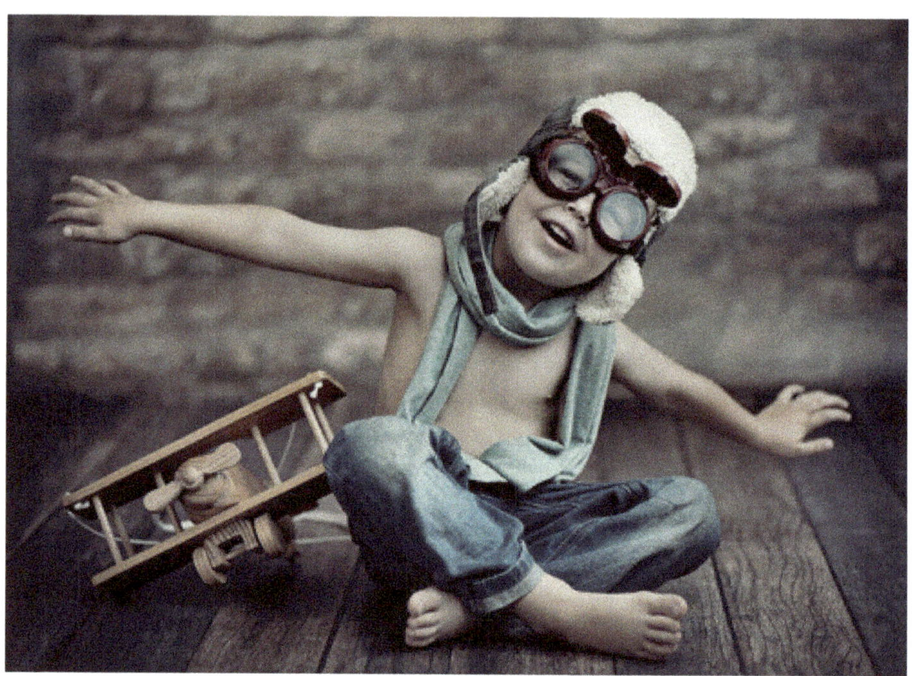

Any list or organization that touches people in marketing, advertising, public relations, or  broadcasting will have leads you can and should follow.

Look in the yellow pages (they still exist!) for manufacturers, especially clothing makers, accessories producers, and cosmetics companies. Small local companies may have a need for catalog work. Catalogs? Sure, any company that produces almost anything locally will need advertising brochures or photography for their catalogs. These may not be your best or first choice leads, but they should not be ignored.

It is important not to forget technology. The Internet is a very powerful marketing tool, but more than that, it is communications tool. No, you are not likely to have people purchase from your site, but it is a place where people can go to see your most recent color photos, catch up on your current credits, and locate your agent or contact information is invaluable.

But the key element to the Internet is the social media aspects. One actress I know has a very busy social media - and she works constantly. She is in Twitter, MySpace, Me.com. IMDB, MyStudio, LinkedIn, Facebook, or nerium. On these sites, she is also a member of different groups, especially the local groups where rumors of open auditions abound. Modeling is not a part-time job.

To be successful, you must be looking for work constantly, exchanging information with friends and other professionals, and getting out, meeting the other working professionals in the field. Sitting at home eating bonbons and watching soaps will not bring any work to your door. It will make you fat, though. Constantly going from one casting potential to another will help keep you fit.

A commercial web site runs about $10-20 a month from a local provider. Some internet service providers offer decent personal home pages with their account. You won't need much, just a few pages of photos, a little text, and contact information. You do not need a shopping basket. If you want, open a PayPal account and link it to your site or use one of the other apps like Selfie that allow you to sell products from your site without the high costs of a merchant account. The web site should be on all you promotional material and it should be updated regularly.

Believe it or not, this is something you can do yourself quickly and easily. Places like FedEx/Kinko's Copies or Alphagraphics will scan photos for a reasonable rate or you can buy an inexpensive printer that will scan at resolutions that are fine for the Internet. National photography finishers have services to scan your photos and send them to you over the internet or on a disk. It is not difficult to find someone on a more personal level who will help, especially if there is a college or tech school in the area, but creating a web page today is as easy as point, click, drag.

One warning about the Internet: put nothing on the site that you would not mind having distributed widely by other people. In other words, nudes or sexy pictures are sure to be "leached" from your site and may appear on underground or porn sites. It does you not good to have your naked body splattered all over the web if your contact information is missing. You want work from your site, not just exposure.

Keep the pictures exciting and interesting, but not something that would interest a porn purveyor enough to add your photo to his or her site. And remember: once on the Internet, it is *always* there somewhere. Be very, very careful what you Tweet or post on social networks. It can kill a career if the wrong person sees that awkward photo. Or worse: it can label you as a target.

Learn where to hang out. Before it closed, the Coffee Plantation in the Biltmore Plaza in Phoenix was the center for the weekend arts community. Actors, artists, and musicians flocked to the location as an impromptu meet-and-greet night. That also drew producers, agents, and managers. It was a good place to meet people, talk shop and make contacts. Go to nearby film festivals.

Meet the independent producers and actors who attend. Find out where they hang out. Go to a community college theatrical performance. Meet and talk to the cast. Open your eyes and look around. The connections you need are all around you. Staying home playing video games is probably not going to help.

And finally, never underestimate personal referrals. When a casting agent is scratching their head looking for someone who might fit a role, the phrase "I know someone who..." from a fellow actor or crewmember can open a lot of doors. That seldom guarantees the job, but it does almost always guarantee an interview. The rest is up to you.

Be creative in your job search. Use all the tools available. It takes hours and hours of work to build a career that will sustain you in a small market. It is not luck or a good agent that will set you up with enough assignments on a weekly basis to earn a living or to make modeling a profitable hobby. Do not be afraid to look outside the box and do not rely on only one or two sources of leads.

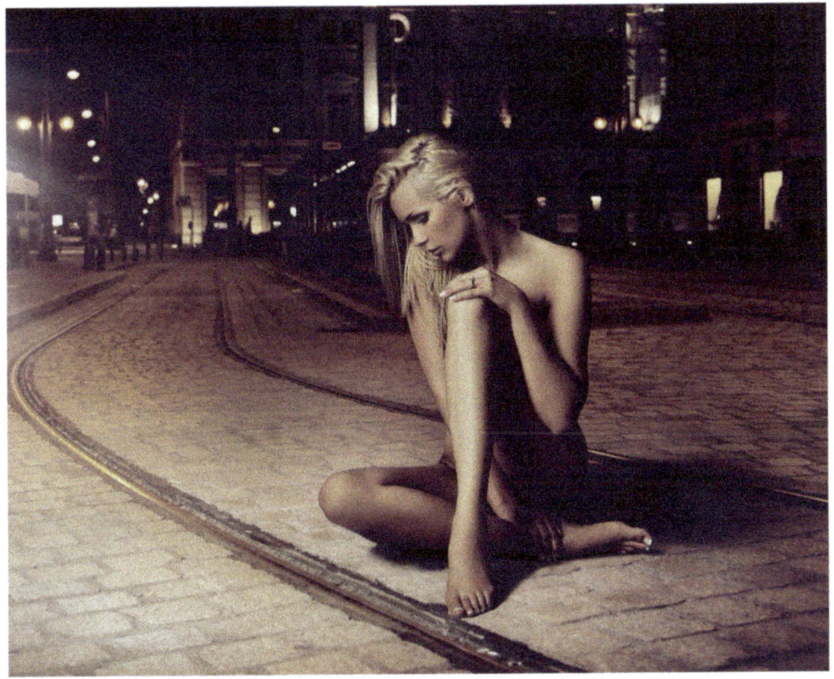

## DO IT YOURSELF

As I mentioned before, the cost of producing videos and slide shows with the Internet has come down tremendously. Quality video can be produced by a small group of friends and uploaded for virtually no money if the equipment is available. This gives the model a potential platform for self generated productions. These can be anything from a talk show, to a fashion slide show, to a video production. Return on your efforts, however, with the Internet is still sketchy. Finding sponsors is not easy, but then again your production costs are so low that you don't need to charge a lot for commercial space, or mentions, or banner ads in order to make profit.

I am not a big fan of short films. Not that I don't enjoy them - some are quite good - but I have never seen much of a commercial value in shorts, beyond serving as a platform for writers and producers to showcase themselves, they also give actresses or actors a vehicle to work on a project that both demonstrates their ability and look and also has - thanks again to the Internet - a good chance of getting wide exposure and making a little money.

For the most part, "little" is very close to none. However, Amazon, iTunes, and other online distributors do provide opportunities for people to distribute their work and make an income. Amazon, Hulu, and NetFlix offer opportunities to sell longer form productions, too. Even YouTube will allow someone to make a few dollars with their advertising. If you look around, there are a number of venues where short work can be exhibited. Where some provide a little income, others offer a way for you to inexpensively demonstrate your creativity and talent. If you want more control over who sees the video, up load it to someplace like Vimeo or Dropbox, where you can store your work and only the people you invite can see it. Take some time and read about *The Guild*. It may give you some ideas.

Why else are you working so hard, so thanklessly, when you could be relaxing with a diet soda?

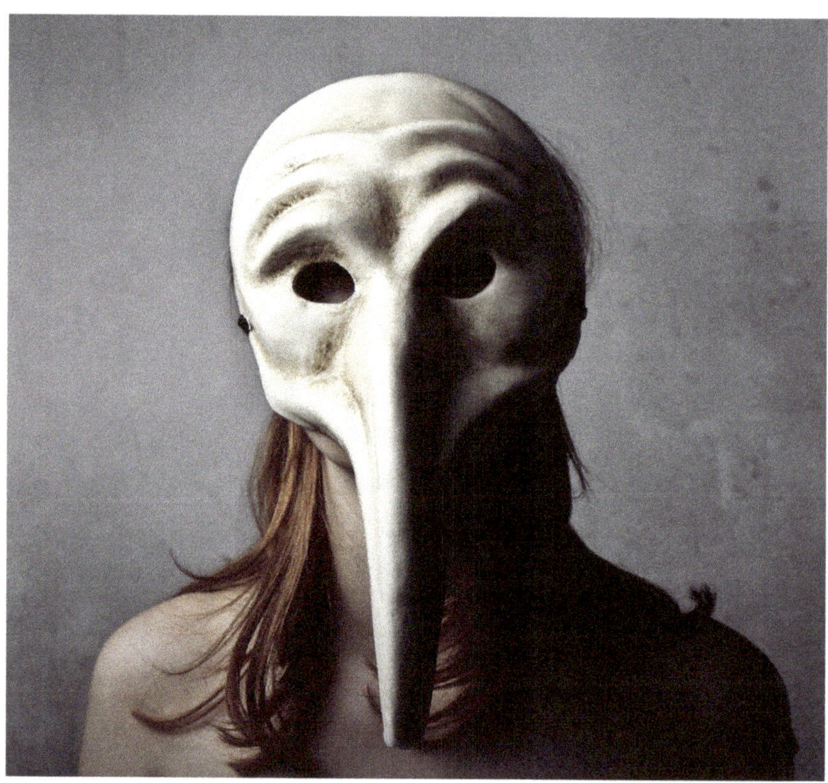

# 4 MAKING THE PITCH

## INTERVIEWS

Be on time.

Be early.

But never, ever, ever, ever, be late.

And, finally, be there 30 minutes early.

***Tip: Late is arriving any time past 15 minutes BEFORE your call time.***

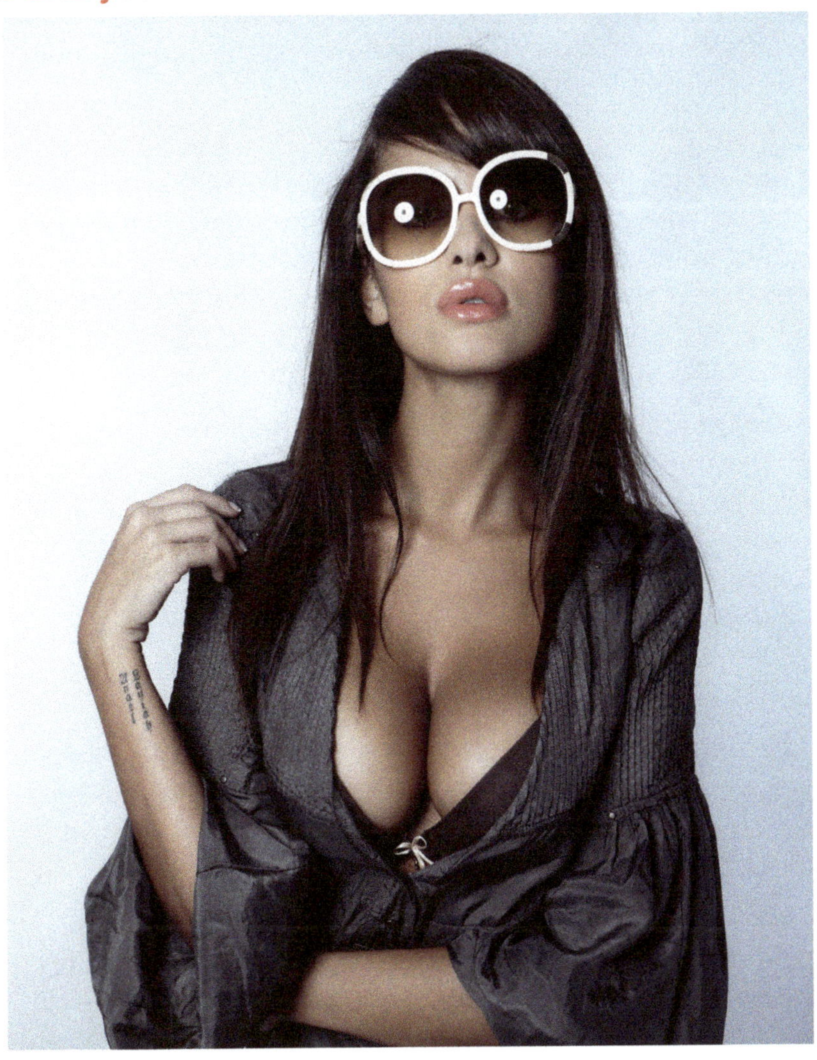

Very seldom will the model find employment without first having to go through the ordeal of an interview. These "trials by fire" are demanding and often nerve-racking. That is if you are unprepared. It is really very simple to breeze through an interview if you know what to expect and you can give the casting person what he/she expects.

Always be polite, well-mannered and honest. Do not ask the ad agency or other client how much money they made last year. In fact, unless asked, it is better not to mention money at all. That is your agent's job. Never smoke or accept a drink in an interview. If offered decline politely, although you may have some water. You're there for business. Keep it that way. And that includes turning down later social offers.

When you arrive, remember, SMILE! A pleasant face is easier to look at than one which is nervous and frightened. Shake hands firmly (unless you are at a cattle call. At that point don't shake hands unless they offer - you may be number 253 for the day) and look the interview in the eye. Do not sit and gaze around the office reading plaques or staring at the wall decorations.

Pay attention to what is being said and asked only those questions which will help keep the interviewer's mind on why you are there: to seek modeling work. That means you're not to discuss your husband or boyfriend or children or current employer. If asked, answer the questions, but be brief! You should be polite, but save the details. Most people are only interested in themselves, anyway.

Learn to sense when the interview is over and do not overstay your welcome. Also, watch little things like how you sit (posture is very important) and what you do with your hands (don't fidget).

While you're waiting for the interviewer to finish looking at your portfolio sit patiently and quietly. If there are derogatory comments made about your photographs, note them mentally but do not let your disappointment show.

Never become defensive. Sometimes, casting agents are rude solely to see how well you stand up to their criticism.

If they ask how you are, only positive responses - it is the wrong time to discuss parking problems or boyfriend issues or a bad hair day, even though that is on the top of your mind.

If you hope to get the part - or another one later - turn your phone OFF.

## THE AUDITION

Sometimes an advertising agency, and almost always a video producer, will require an audition for a specific

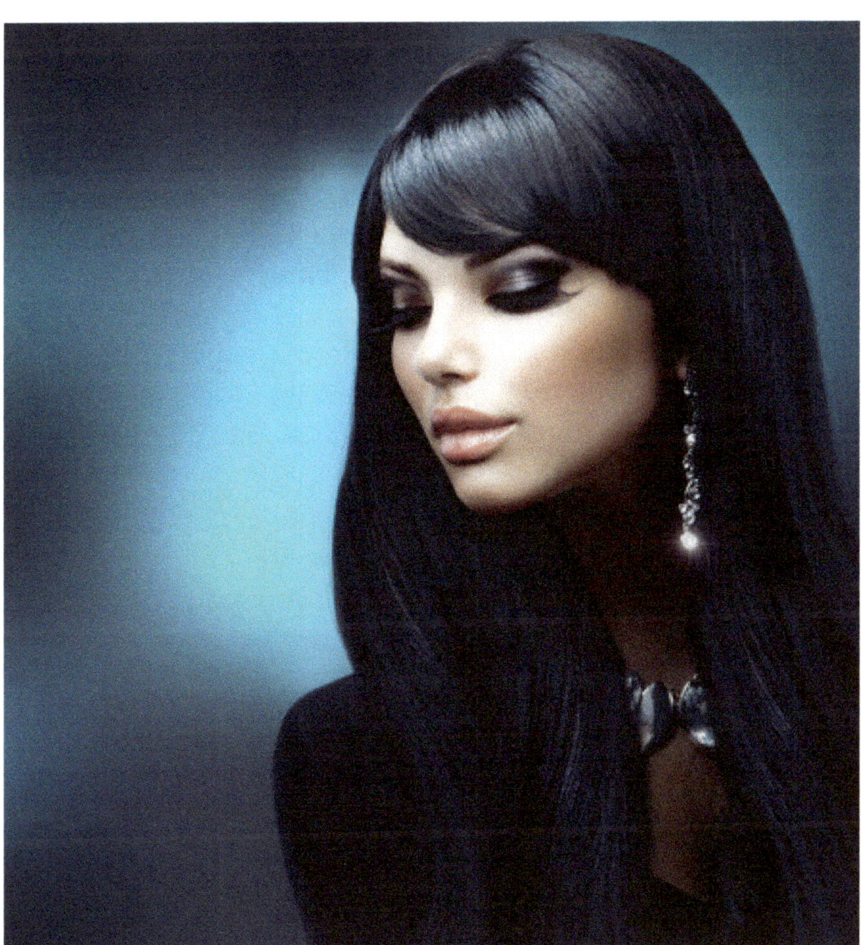

production. If you are not handed a specific script, then you should have something prepared. That means a memorized monologue and a 30 or 60 second commercial. The total time taking in presenting the samples of your ability should not exceed three minutes but a two-minute showing is best. It does not take long to bore a producer who has had to sit through 20 or 30 auditions before you arrived.

If you are handed a "side" (a short segment of the script), you may be expected to read it cold. If you cannot read cold scripts out loud, then you may as well forget television and radio commercials. Even if you can memorize well, you may not be given the chance at the audition. Learn to read well out loud and expand your vocabulary so you can pick up any document and read it the first time as if you had it memorized.

If you are given a prepared script and asked to look it over, memorize it! It does not take much skill or talent to memorize a 60 second spot. It is rather easy. This is something you can practice at home. Copy down the dialogue from radio ads and then put them aside for a couple weeks. Later, pick them up, look them over three to five times, and put the paper down or give it to a friend. Then do the commercial as much from memory as you can. The more you do this the easier it becomes. Later, try cold readings memorized from plays and film scripts. With practice, it is not difficult.

Make choices on how to present your script. Be confident if your choices. If they do not like your choice, they will ask you to read it another way. If you are successful, you have a shot. Never apologize for how you chose to read the script.

***Tip: Do not be impatient with waiting. It may be a drag, but waiting on "them" is better than having "them" wait on you... even if you are established and a "star."***

Don't mess with props or movement unless directed to do so. Do not expect direction, but be willing to take it.

Learn how to stand still in front of the camera.

Say as little as you can. From the moment you step in the room you are auditioning. Don't ask if you should sit, stand, or wall (stand unless told otherwise); don't ask how others have done; don't ask if the producer or director is there; don't make any kind of excuses; don't complain about how long you have had to read over the side. Just go in, be polite, thank them and go.

Do not be afraid to make mistakes, but never be afraid to ask for proper pronunciation before you start. If the dialogue calls for a smile, keep the smile no matter what happens. If you mispronounce a word keep going. If you forget a line, learn to improvise. Never stop in the middle of a commercial and panic. Do not roll your eyes, look away, or exclaim "Oh, s--t!" (And yes, that is a real-life example.) That is unprofessional and it eliminates a lot of promising talent in the beginning.

Keep going until you reach the end. Never make excuses. Bring none of your issues to the audition.

If you did a poor job, asked the director if you can do it again. If they were impressed by your ability to maintain character they may allow you another shot. While you might not get the lead you may potentially land of supporting spot.

When they ask if you have any questions, it is rhetorical. That is the same as asking if you are ready.

At the audition remember: never break character, do not stop in the middle of the spot, and be ready for either a script or to present a prepared monologue. Video ads pay the model the most money and offer the best chance of her "being discovered." Concentrate improving your talents before the camera. This is one time when using a cell phone for practice can be very, very handy.

Remember, when you go to an audition, you are there to *work*, not socialize! Even if you don't feel that your three minute interview was work, it sure was for someone who may have sat through 300 others that day. Even if all you do is walk in, twirl once, and leave, make it the best audition you have and be happy you have it.

Interviews and auditions can be scary things. Do the best you can with the fear. Turn it to your advantage. Take that adrenalin - the increased heart rate and tense muscles - and put energy into your audition. Make a mental connection that this is the way you feel when you succeed - embrace the fear as a precursor to success. And finally, what is the worst that can happen if you don't get the job? Move on. Another one is waiting. Stop telling *yourself* no just because someone else said it for an assignment. Push out the negativity.

If you blow an audition or interview, do not compound it by making the other errors we have discussed here. There will be another chance if you stay professional. NOT getting an assignment is sometimes a good thing.

## GRAMMAR

While we're talking about talking, it is amazing how many models should never have been allowed to graduate from freshman English. Grammar and proper speech patterns are a big part of how well you will impress the interviewer.

Here are some of the biggest offenders:

1. Where are you located at? (The "at" is a dangling participle and is used in common slang. It lowers your perceived educational level to almost moron.)

2. What's it about? (What's what about? Make your questions specific and direct. Do not use implied subjects. And guess what: about is a dangling participle.)

3. I seen your ads on the television. (I saw your ads. Learn the proper use of verbs.)

4. "I am bringing my television to the repair shop." (The person who wrote that for a TV commercial should have used proper grammar. "I am taking…" To properly use "bring" or "take," you must know whether the object is being moved toward or away from the

subject. If toward, use "bring." If away, use "take." Your agent will tell you to *take* the side with you, the casting director will tell you to *bring* it. Learn the meaning of common words.)

5. "I don't have no photographs." (Two things: one is the double negative "don't" and "no" and the other is the use of "no" in this context. "I don't have any..." and if you don't have photos, then you shouldn't be there.)

6. "I just want to axe how much I'm making for this." (Nothing. If you cannot pronounce words properly at the interview, chances are good you won't pronounce them properly in front of the camera.) These are examples of actual casting sessions. Needless to say, if the producer is not impressed with your vocabulary, enunciation, or your word choice, the producer is not likely to cast you in a production that has his reputation riding on the outcome. Here some more common mistakes. Do you recognize yourself making any of these?

7. Anxious - To be "anxious" implies a fear or dread. It doesn't mean you're looking forward to something. That word is "eager."

8. Farther and Further - The word "farther" implies a measurable distance. "Further" should be reserved for abstract lengths you can't always measure.

9. Fewer and Less - "Less" is reserved for hypothetical quantities. "Few" and "fewer" are for things you can quantify.

10. Lay and Lie - "Lay" is a transitive verb. It requires a direct subject and one or more objects. Its present tense is "lay" (e.g., I lay my head on a pillow) and its past tense is "laid" (e.g., I laid the paper on the table). "Lie" is an intransitive verb. It needs no object. Its present tense is "lie" (e.g., The choices lie between hard and very hard) and its past tense is "lay" (e.g., The starlet lay waiting for attention). The most com-

mon mistake occurs with the past tense of the transitive "lay" (e.g., I laid on the bed) when the intransitive past tense of "lie" (e.g., I lay on the bed) would be appropriate.

11. May and Might - "May" implies a possibility. "Might" implies far more uncertainty.

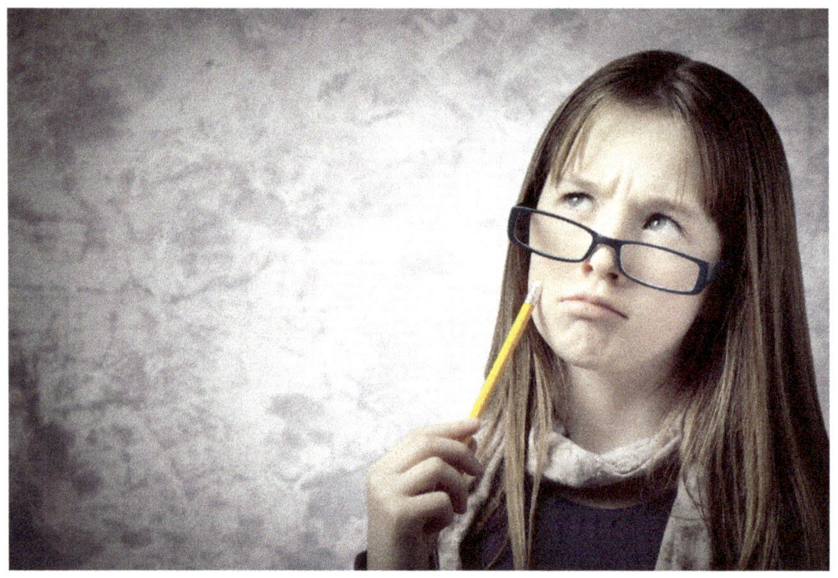

12. Whether and If - "Whether" is *not* interchangeable with "if." It isn't. "Whether" expresses a condition where there are two or more alternatives. "If" expresses a condition where there are no alternatives.

13. Which and That - "That" is a restrictive pronoun. It's vital to the noun to which it refers. "Which" introduces a relative clause. It allows qualifiers that may not be essential.

14. Who and Whom - "Who" is a subjective pronoun, along with "he," "she," "it," "we," and "they." It's used when the pronoun acts as the subject of a clause. "Whom" is an objective pronoun, along with "him," "her," "it", "us," and "them." Use whom when the pronoun acts as the object of a clause. Using "who" or "whom" depends on whether you're referring to the subject or object of a sentence.

These are just a few the common examples which perspective models use every day. In the interviews which I conducted, only about one out of 25 models escaped without making at least one of these errors, and usually they make more. Items five and six are automatic rejects regardless of talent or looks. The others require careful consideration. You must impress the interviewer with your ability and your intelligence. If you cannot speak properly in the interview, then you will not be seriously considered for a position and you will never see the opportunity to make a successful national television commercial.

A few more things to remember:

You must always be prepared but not over-prepared. You might think you are going in to audition for a catalogue spread for evening wear when they say you would be great for the sports line. Be flexible.

Ask questions if you are unsure. Take directions. Be willing to do what they ask - in reason. If they ask you to strip for anything that is not clearly stated up front as a nude or semi-nude shot, don't hesitate: leave.

Otherwise, attitude pays.

Always dress for the role. If it is high fashion, a dress and heels, but not club wear. If it is sportswear, more casual. I always recommend a skirt over slacks. Work with jewel tones, solid colors or simple palters, v-necks, and light make-up.

Since you were on time, and confident in your ability, show it! Be self-assured! Act as if you assume you are the right person - not arrogant, just comfortable. Make a strong entrance, shake hands firmly, and after the audition, thank them, make sure they have a current headshot, and leave without hesitation.

## APPEARANCE

The way you look at an interview is by no means at the least important item in selling yourself to a casting director. This is your first impression. It supersedes your photographs in your audition. It even precedes your opportunity to talk. Take the hint: be extra careful of your appearance when going job hunting.

Your dress should always be neat and clean. It does not need to be fancy, but it does need to reflect your desire to be considered professional. That means no jeans, shorts, halter tops, T-shirts, or other common daily wear items. Males should be dressed in sports clothes of conservative cut and fabric or conservative suits.

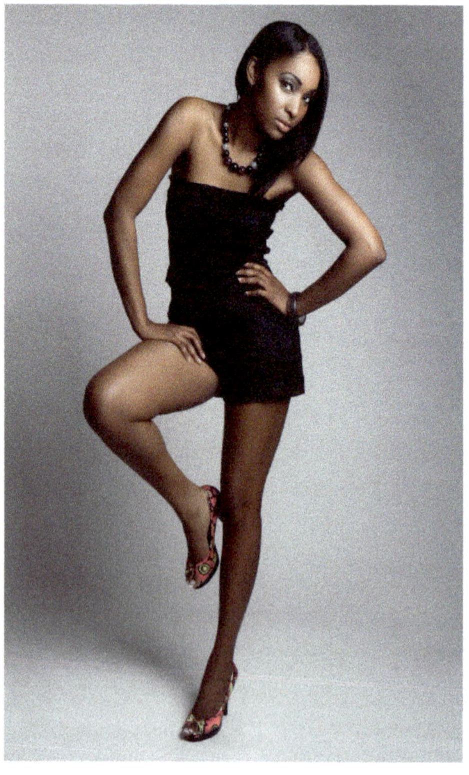

Women should wear dresses or skirt outfits. No long dresses and never MIDI dresses - just above or below the knee is the proper length for skirts. Super sexy cut tops should also be avoided. You're trying to sell your talent not your body even though your body is a lot of part of what they're going to be buying. You're only using your looks on your go-see (to "go see" the casting people for a non-audition meeting) to get them moderately interested but not as a final selling point.

***Tip: Women, in particular, need to be aware of how their clothes fit and what shows when they move.***

Makeup on women should be very light. Use only

enough to accent your best features (and perhaps a light cover-up). You're not going to a club or to a high fashion assignment. Use subtle tones on the eyes and a light blush. Lipstick should match the blush and not be overdone. Use a lip gloss, however, as moist lips are more attractive than dry ones.

Men should not use makeup for interviews. They should, however, be aware of proper application procedures should they be required to use makeup on assignment where make-up people may be too busy with the women.

While styles change almost daily, there are certain basic rules which should be observed on all models. Facial complexion is very important. A clear complexion is vital for any model because hi-def images show every blemish and bump.

***Tip: It is true that cameras add weight. In photography and video, good trim figures are required.***

By using a little common sense, by maintaining proper hygiene and good grooming standards every day, the model should be ready for most assignments, even those which come with only a moment's notice.

One note about tattoos: they have become very popular but they can be highly detrimental to a novice model's career, especially if they are where they're likely to be seen in normal clothing. There is the argument that tattoos can be covered up, but that is seldom effective with high-definition video or still photos. I can say with absolute certainty that tattoos have cost a lot of actors and models potentially lucrative assignments. While it may be tempting to paint your body, remember that is your stock in trade and what you put on it may highly limit your desirability for a large number of potential clients.

## WHAT TO DO AFTER THE AUDITION

Once you have been to a casting, your job is far from over. You just walked out of the room and chances are they already forgot who you are. Here are a few things you can do to keep your name in front of the casting director that, believe it or not, actually work:

1. As soon as you get home, send a thank you note. It doesn't matter if it's an e-mail or a card, but a short message of gratitude is always appreciated. In this case, you get more with handwritten cards - unless your handwriting is as bad as mine. Bright colors, incidentally, very often end up pinned on the wall. And guess who they think about every time they see it?

Remember to always include links to your online material. However, never, never ever, send a card or note and ask for anything back. Do not request an evaluation, or information on how a casting went, or anything else. Just say thank you and be done. Ask another time. Believe it or not casting directors are some of the few people who really are as busy as they think they are.

2. Set up a spreadsheet that includes the date, time, casting director, project, and the results would call. Make note of any names of important people at the casting. Write down if they prefer a follow-up by e-mail or snail mail. Set up a tickler column to remind yourself when to get back with the agent. Contacting an agent more frequently than six weeks can hurt you more than help you.

3. Check with the casting director, and if it's okay with them, and you have some talent with writing, put out a monthly or bimonthly newsletter. Send it by e-mail and only if they agree to receive the e-mail. Make it light, make it funny, drop in a little information that may not be readily available, but most of all keep it short and spiffy. It's a good chance including a photo, a link to a new reel, or an update on something else you are doing in the industry. Just be very careful not to overdo it. And whatever you do, do not start posting personal items on the casting director's Facebook

page or other social media outlet.

4. If you are doing something in the arts, send a casting director an invitation. Of course, make sure you're inviting them to something worth seeing. You might be great, but if the rest of your theater company stinks, you're not going to leave a good impression and you will have wasted the casting director's time. Not a good decision.

5. Make something. Get together with other professionals and create a 2-3 minute show case of your work - interacting on the runway, a TV commercial, a clip from a movie, something that shows you can work with others.

Casting directors are not managers or agents. Keep your interaction brief, professional, and to the point. That doesn't mean you shouldn't focus on building collaborative relationships; but casting directors are not responsible for helping you develop your own career. Communicate but do none of it in excess.

## THE POWER OF NO

It is easy to get down after hearing "No" a few dozen - hundred - times. It is part of the business. You can't help but feel the rejection. It can eat at you and make you doubt yourself. Most successful models have even lost jobs after they were cast simply because someone they had never met decided they wanted a different "look." That is not your fault. It is outside your control. Sometimes it is stupid, illogical, and just wrong. But it cannot be allowed to slow you down or stop you. Not, at least, if you really want to succeed.

"No" can also bring on a struggle with self-esteem. You know you are beautiful - under the lights and before the camera, even if you believe you are plain everywhere else. You know you have talent. When you hear "No" over and over, you begin to wonder what is wrong with yourself. Be honest. The answer is probably nothing. There is absolutely nothing you can do if the casting call fits you to a 'T' and the client walks in and decides he absolutely has to have the mongrel sitting at the donut shop down the block. You always do your best, you are always professional; the rest is out of your hands.

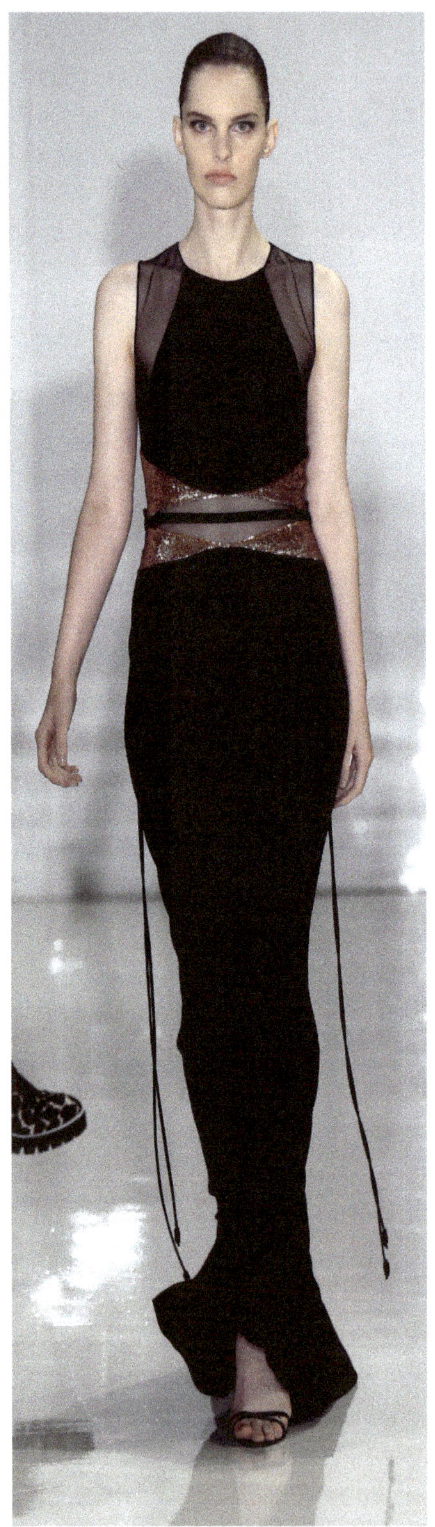

"No" can rob you of your confidence. "No" can create self-doubt. "No" can create hesitation. But it is just a word. You will hear it 100 times for every "Yes."

"No" does not necessarily mean that you were not right, not pretty, not good enough, for the job. Unless you really do need to improve your acting skills (even models "act" with their expressions), all "No" means is that out of the 500 other applicants, one more closely fit what they wanted for height, weight, eye color, hair, or whatever. Don't let "No" get in your way.

# 5 ON ASSIGNMENT

## THE TIME CLOCK

No matter what the assignment, arrive 15 to 30 minutes early. This will be on your own time unless the photographer or producer is ready early. Then they will appreciate your consideration.

Be prepared to say as long as it takes and never leave until released. This is an economical rule of thumb: if the model arrives late then the producer may have to pay extra for the crew, or the photographer, or rented props, or lights, or other production tools. A consistently late model is one who will find herself consistently without work.

When you arrive on assignment you must be prepared for overtime. If the call is 7 AM until 1 PM do not plan anything until much later that evening. If things go wrong (and they almost always will) it will take longer to finish the shot than planned. You will be expected to be on location until the shoot is over.

No matter how important a later meeting is to you, it is only secondary to the producer, if he cares at all. You should never leave a production until it is over. The client will generally pay to reshoot with another model than have to call the entire crew back just to reshoot a few seconds of a model who had to leave early.

You may also mark that client off your callback list. Sometimes leaving early may even result in not being paid or in being sued for the additional cost of reshooting.

Models that develop the reputation of being unreliable will lose assignments despite their talent. Clients do not have the time or money to play around with models who cannot behave in a professional manner.

Too many other models are asking for that same job to worry about the one who puts the job second. There is almost never a case where only one model can do a specific job. So remember, the producers always have a choice, there is always someone waiting in the wings.

## BRING IT ALL – AND THEN SOME

If you're providing your own wardrobe, remember the accessories. Belts, jewelry, shoes, and hair products are your responsibility. If you forget the shoes, you may have to purchase some on the spot. Or if the shooting is scheduled when the stores are closed in may be in a lot of trouble, especially if you keep a $500 an hour crew waiting for you go back home to get what you forgot.

Also, take all of your makeup and hair styling material with you. You may need them should the director or photographer call for different look. Usually you'll be told in advance what to wear and what to bring. Do not rely on possible faulty communications in something so vital is your career. When in doubt take it with you. Certainly always be prepared to put your hair up or take it down and to change your make-up style.

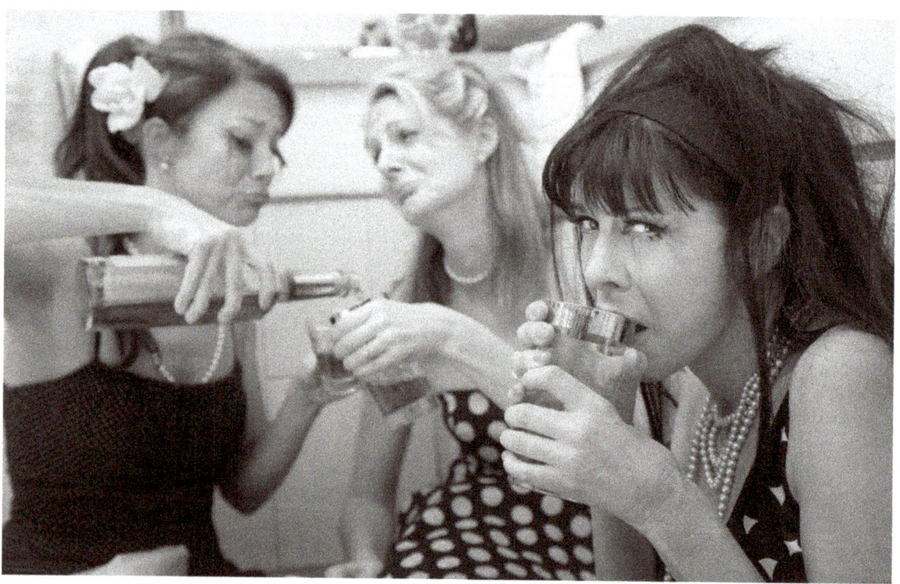

## SMOKING, DRINKING, AND DRUGS

This shouldn't have to be said, but it is something a lot of models forget: no smoking, no drinking, and no drugs on the set or the assignment. One model relates a story about accepted a drink from the photographer at his studio. What was it going to hurt? Generally, nothing. This time, however, the girl was sexually abused because the photographer slipped something into her drink before giving it to her. She was too ashamed after to file a report. Another model lost her steady job with a monthly fashion show by taking too many drinks after the show. She became very... "happy" and loud and was fired for making too much of a scene. It can happen to you if you're not very careful.

Accepting any alcohol or drug on assignment lowers a model's standing from professional to party girl. You're there for business, not for play. Keep it that way. You might miss out on a party or two, but you'll maintain your professional integrity and potentially stay out of life-threatening situations. You certainly will avoid a lot of abuse.

Thirty years ago it was common for the model to bed down with the casting director or producer. This is no longer the case in the US. It is the model's job to see that old habits and not revived. Keep it professional. Always.

***Tip: When on a foreign assignment it is even more important that the model maintain careful control. Many cultures still consider models prostitutes and a careless model can easily end up in a situation she may regret... forever.***

As for smoking, it is not physically dangerous in the same way as taking drinks or drugs. However, it is a well-known fact that smoking decreases lung capacity and this is a disastrous problem for long video or radio speeches. Smoking also conjures up certain social emotional responses to maintain your professional image, it is best not to associate yourself with the subliminal associations conjured up by smoking.

Remember too, smoking yellows the teeth, wrinkles the eyes, and stains fingers. Modeling is a world of images. The model who creates the best image works the most.

***Tip: To many people, smoking is not a sign of sophistication but an advertisement that you are available and willing with low standards.***

At the risk of being called an old fuddy-duddy, I highly recommend that models avoid after-hours social events as much as possible. While it is good business to go to a party and network or to stop off at a bar where the crew is having a drink after work, it is also a way to create more problems than it solves. When attending social events, be very careful of the number of drinks at you take, avoid the drugs, and don't make a spectacle of yourself.

Too many times have I seen good talent go to waste because the model was considered a party girl and not a professional. Modeling is not as much fun as most girls think it is. It takes constant vigilance, a constant eye on image, to maintain a career that is more than a flash in the pan. It requires a lot more self-discipline than almost any other profession.

It is very important that you keep control of your life. It you don't, it becomes easy for your career - or other people - to own you.

Turning down an assignment may not hurt you at all. It may bring respect and more jobs. Or past due notices on the rent. You are the only one who can choose but choose wisely.

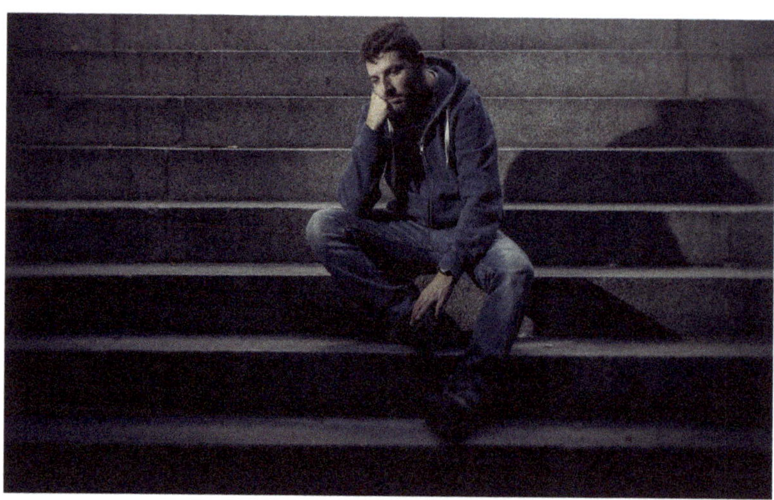

# 6 BETWEEN ASSIGNMENT SURVIVAL

## THE REGULAR JOB

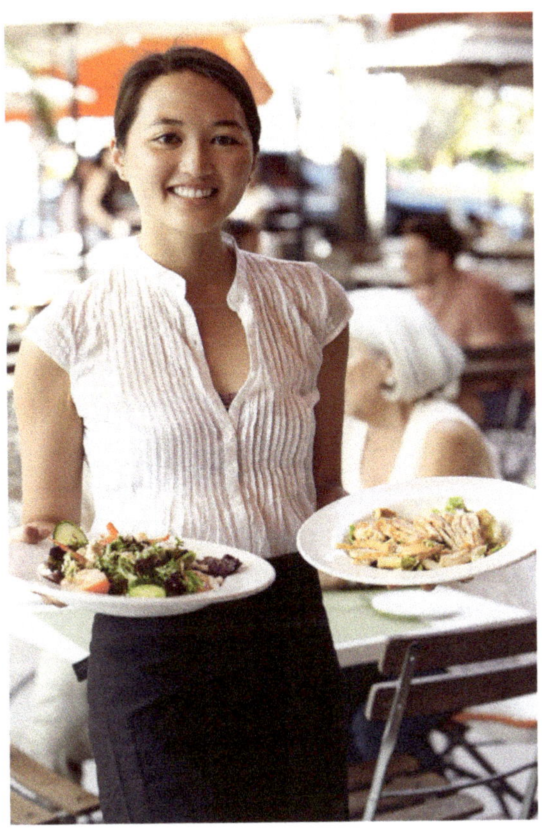

If the model does not have an agent, then she must have the time free during the day to meet with as many producers and casting agents as possible. Well truth be told, she even needs that time with an agent. While some of the pressure is absorbed by the agent and an agent allows a model to find other employment during the day, the model must be available for interviews and assignments when they are held, not when it's convenient for her. If she is not available when the audition is held she shall not be working as a model.

A night job is advantageous for models, someplace where she has the ability to meet people. Any gregarious model who can talk to people easily can frequently find work from her customers - or at least make better tips. Good jobs for models are hard to find. If an employer is properly approached however, good jobs can sometimes be created. No matter where a model works, it is essential that weekday hours the available for interviews and that off time for assignments can be arranged.

That a job (full or part-time) is necessary does not occur to many models. They seem to forget the photography is expensive and that printing composites are equally expensive. That these tools are required before the model lands her first job is also often overlooked. Furthermore, most models do not realize that they are in business for themselves and that, like any new business, it will take months or even years before modeling will be profitable enough for them to live on their modeling income without other means of support.

## OTHER SOURCES

Of course, it is always nice to be independently wealthy or to have someone support you in your career. Generally, however, this is not the case and basic living expenses must be met while the model is building a reliable, high paying clientele.

Should the model be fortunate enough not to require a lot of extra income, then there are still many ways to earn between major assignments. Again, these take work to find and usually require mailing out composites to various companies. However, here are a few tips that might fill the gap between actual modeling jobs:

1. Look for companies doing conventions or exhibition work. They will sometimes use demonstrators and the pay is fairly good. Check the local convention bureau or the Chamber.

2. Cosmetic companies often hire demonstrators to display their products in stores. The pay is usually minimum but sometimes there are commissions.

3. Large hotels and resorts use models for conventions and sometimes fashion shows.

4. Look for grand openings, new home or car shows. They sometimes use models as hostesses.

5. Register with a temp agency if you have the basic secretarial skills; this will allow you to choose

when you want to work and the pay is adequate.

6. Check into teaching modeling makeup or acting techniques at local private modeling schools. These places usually do not have educational requirements if you have experience. If you have some education combined with experience, try your local community college for noncredit classes. The pay and the references are better.

7. Amusement parks often have acting troops which present local melodramas, gunfights, and so on. It is low pay, but good experience and exposure and sometimes they take on additional hosting help.

8. There are an increasing number of ways to earn money on the internet, which require minimal investment and allow the model set her own hours (I do not, however, recommend becoming an on camera model for Internet surfers).

The model must keep ahead of the bill collector without totally consuming the work week. The "dumb blonde model" images disappeared with the dumb blonde. Today's economy calls for a well-educated, sharp model. There are too many economic factors involved to allow for mistakes on the model's part; furthermore; she must be able to meet the demands of the economy in her personal life if she hopes to have the time and money to promote her career. A model, even with a supportive spouse, needs to be in a position to go to assignments and accept work when they come along. If not, even the most supportive spouse will weary of spending money on her hobby.

If you are working for a video production or a photo shoot for a larger corporation, it is likely that you will need to sign a time card. Most often this is a multi-part form and you should receive a copy. The company will send a check to you or your agent within a specified time frame. It is a good idea to check how your hours will be recorded when booked or at least when you first arrived.

As a talent agent, all my models had a small stack of booking tickets. These were filled in and signed for every non-union assignment (unions have their own forms that work just fine). I insisted these be complete and signed even if the company had their own time cards. This way I could track their work and if there was any question about the pay, I had back-up documentation. Independent models should do the same thing. It is much easier to argue about hours when there is a signed document available than when it is one word against another.

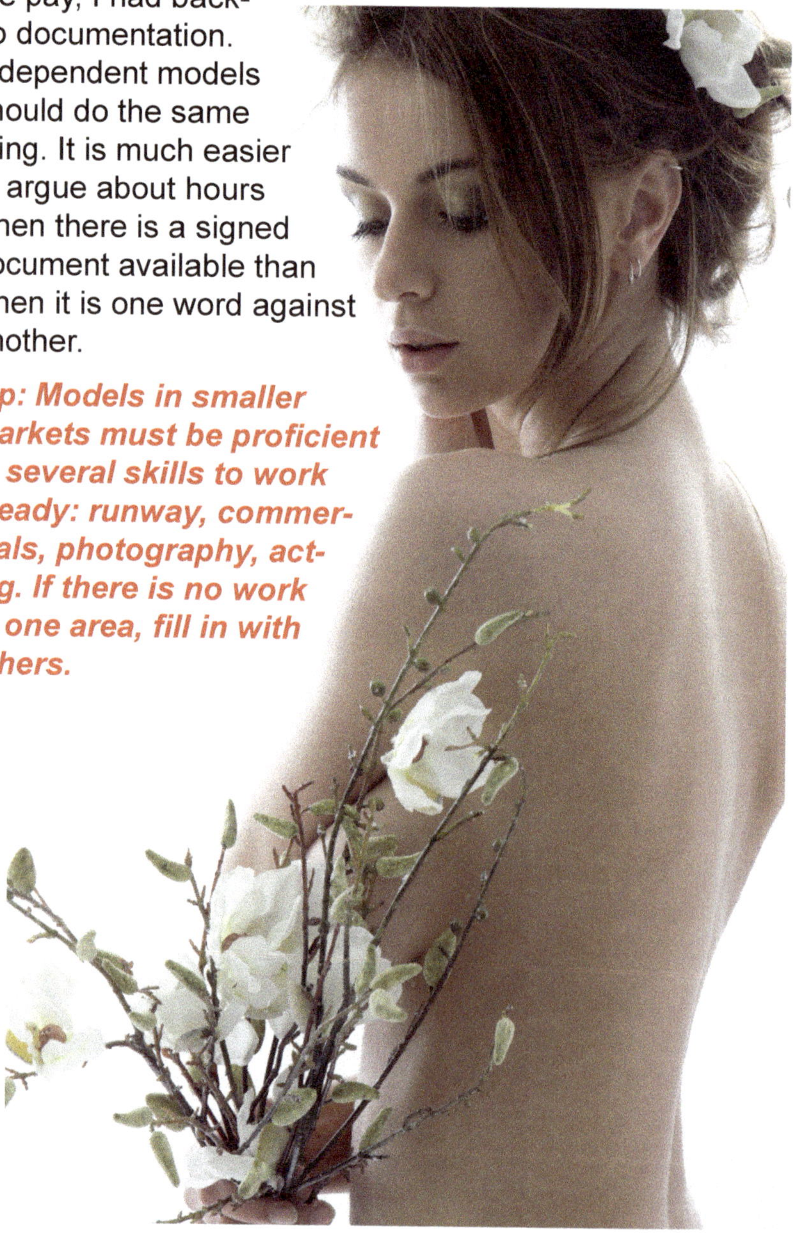

***Tip: Models in smaller markets must be proficient in several skills to work steady: runway, commercials, photography, acting. If there is no work in one area, fill in with others.***

# 7 LEGALITIES

## COPYRIGHT

Sometimes a novice model feels she has the right to determine which photographs taken of her may be used and which may not. Except in extreme cases were such rights are included in the contract, the model has no say at all concerning the use of her photographs. Usually, the person who is paying for the assignment has all rights to all photographs. This holds true under certain circumstances even if a release is not signed. Once the model has accepted a fee for her work she has acknowledged the release of that work.

So, be careful what you sign. If you're only giving rights for promotional or personal use, make sure that all copies of the releases stipulate such; and if something is added in, make sure the photographer initials that section.

If you signed a blanket release, the photographer has the right to use your photographs in any way he chooses. That means reselling them and not paying you any extra. It also means that he can use these photographs anyway he or she chooses without asking your permission. Generally, this is not a big problem in working for an advertising agency, professional photographer, or establish video producer. It *can* be a problem, when you are working with people who are on the fringes of the industry – students, beginning photographers, and the many sleaze bags in the industry.

Also, when you're working in exchange for prints for an independent photographer, be extra careful. It is not unusual for the photographer to demand the release be signed before the shooting starts. That is all right as photographers often forget the paperwork later. So always be aware of how you are posing. After a shoot, some model's may have a suddenly change of heart and a lot of time and effort is wasted on photographs that cannot be used without a release. If you sign before the shooting, then know how you are posing and do not do any poses without being sure that you would not mind those shots being publicized. It is very easy for model be talked into a compromising situation and regret it later.

***Tip: With digital photography and the Internet, anything you do in front of a camera can quickly become public knowledge. Be aware of what is being taken.***

Generally speaking, the model should not expect to be allowed the right to approve the final edit on a television ad, editorial approval on a film, or the selection of the final print of a photograph. The time and effort consumed here is financially prohibitive to allow the model that much control. Besides, the shot you hate the most may well be the best one for the purpose for which you were hired.

It is also important for the model to know that she has chosen a career which makes her a "public figure." What that means is that you, as a model, have chosen a career which is designed to put you before the public. You're seeking publicity of yourself. Therefore, if a photographer should take a photograph of you doing anything in a public place, he may use that photograph without your permission under most conditions. He can certainly post it online if he wants. That may even apply if he's photographing in the studio or on location and he catches you unaware. That all boils down to a simple statement: be careful what you sign and more careful what you do.

## MODEL RELEASES

Almost every modeling assignment requires a release. If the model is under the legal age, a parent or legal guardian has to co-sign the release. Sometimes an agent will be given a limited "power of attorney" for this purpose. Otherwise, your legal guardian will have to be present for at least part of the shot. If you're underage, it is probably a good idea to have a responsible individual of legal age at the assignment. It is too easy for young models to get caught up in the excitement and glamour associated with modeling and acting. It is too easy to make a naive mistake. There are many examples, but look at the Roman Polanski case before leaving a youngster alone on location.

Assignment release forms come in many different styles but they are all basically the same. You give up our rights to the photographs, films, videotapes, etc. made of you for all time or for limited time in exchange for "value" received - money or prints usually. It also specifies,

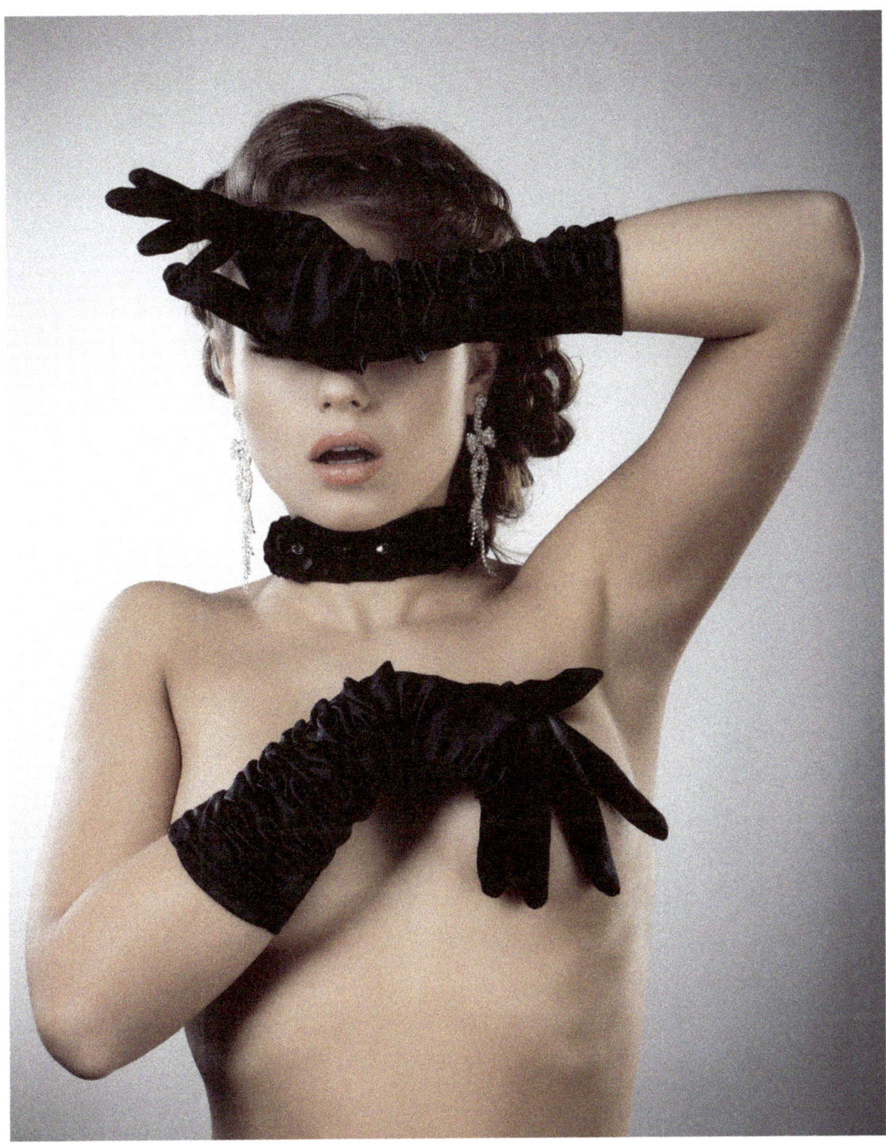

sometimes, when and where those photographs may be used. If no such provisions are made and there is no provision for residual payments and royalties you can expect only the initial payment. Make sure you know what the work is being used for and protect your future income by limiting the release if it seems advisable.

***Tip: What the photographer sees and what the camera sees are not always the same. worry about what the camera sees and records, not the photographer.***

Many releases are considered "boilerplate". Photographers by them in packs from photo stores or print them from an online source. These are usually rather ambiguous and turn over all rights to the photographer. Make sure you read what you sign. Make sure you understand what you read. The Internet provides ample opportunity for one mistake on your part to go viral.

## BUYOUTS, RESIDUALS, & ROYALTIES

For our purposes here, royalties and residuals will mean the same thing: any monies paid for uses of a talent's efforts after the initial use period. For most media contracts, the initial agreement is a minimum of 13 weeks. That means the company has a right to use your image as often as they wish for 13 weeks. At the end of that time they must either stop using your work or pay an additional fee. There may also be provisions for preventing you from modeling for a competing firm during that time. If so, you should be paid more. Print contracts may also be for a limited time although generally, and especially for local publication, once the model is paid she can expect no additional income - called a "buyout."

A lot of companies, especially a small advertising agency or a small retailer, will prefer a one year buyout or a total buyout. This gives them unlimited use of your work for up to one year or forever. Usually, this provides a substantial discount over the use cost of individual thirteen week contracts. At the end of the year, you're either paid again or the company stops using your work. It is only in a few instances that a commercial runs longer than two years, though some commercials have a much longer life, especially if they are earmarked for specific season, like Christmas.

Occasionally, the model might run into a company that demands a total, unlimited buyout of the talent's work. It is generally inadvisable to allow the company to use your likeness in their advertising on an unlimited basis. Look closely at the project use and audience and balance that against the compensation.

If you feel that it will only receive limited, local exposure, then such a deal may not be too bad. In most cases, however, you should always limit the available time in which a company can use your work for advertising purposes.

This does not hold true for releases for photographers who use their work in their portfolios or for some other noncommercial work. Such releases may be without time limits. In any case, if they want a total buy-out, your fee should be substantially higher than normal.

For a good idea on how and why and when a model should ask for residual payments and when she should accept the straight buyout for media work, she should again contact the local SAG/AFTRA office. As a rule, the union people are not too upset with nonunion models and actors who are working on a local level if they try to maintain the same rates and standards as the union members. In markets like Los Angeles and New York, nonunion models and actors are very seldom used for broadcast work. In the smaller markets that have less national business, the union affiliation is less important.

While I do not recommend joining the union if you live outside NY or LA until you are forced to, it should be noted that a model has a much better chance of obtaining national broadcast advertising assignments (which may pay up to $30,000 for a single day's work with minimal residuals) than she has if is she is nonunion. For print advertising, there are no union guidelines, but those in broadcast still form a good foundation for negotiation. Ultimately, if you're working at this level, you really should have an agent do all the negotiations for you.

If, at any time a model feels that the money owed her for advertising or film work is not being paid, she generally has right to request an audit of the producer's books. This audit is at her expense if nothing is found to be amiss. However, if the model is being shorted, she can then asked for the money owed, the audit fees, and any court fees included. In a case where there is any question, the model is best advised to seek a lawyer who is knowledgeable in copyright and contract negotiations. Outside of Los Angeles and New York however lawyers who specialize in media are few and far between.

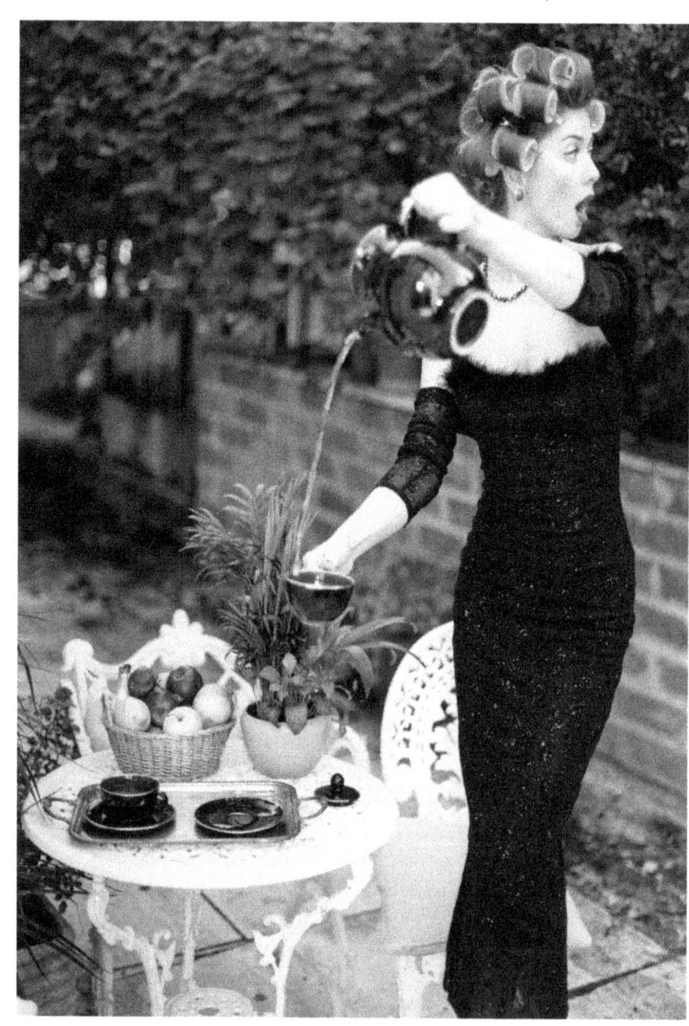

Royalties can also be obtained when the contract limits the use of the number of times an ad is run. Such a contract usually provides a client with the uncontested right to use the ad as often and as many different medias he chooses so long as an additional fee is paid for each additional market/magazine/time period in which the ad is used.

When the model begins negotiation for royalties and buyouts on the national level, she should either engage a lawyer or an agent. She should do this for local work too, but the stakes for national or international work are so much higher that it can be very costly to make a mistake.

These types of contracts can often be sticky and have to be worded in strange ways that the average person has a difficult time comprehending. Sometimes, the convoluted language can disguise the real content, which can be damaging to the model. The beginning model will probably be dealing with straight buyouts for local market which is usually unlimited or a year's rights or flat hourly or session rate with no residuals.

I always recommend an agent or lawyer handle contract negotiations. Quite frankly, models, actors, and any other artist starving for work is more likely to give away the store than to negotiate a good rate.

## TAXES

Since the model is in essence self-employed, there is a realm of complications involved with filling out tax returns. There are a few basic deductible items that the model should be aware of and of which she should maintain records. In the first few years there may be a net loss of the entire year, but hang in there and you'll soon see a profit; even with all of these deductions:

1. This book, and others like it, are deductible as reference and business publications.

2. Clothes purchased, especially for an assignment and the dry cleaning bill for any clothing you use which is not reimbursed by the client for specific assignment.

3. Gas and certain travel expenses. 4. Make up used *exclusively* for modeling jobs.

5. Photography, composites, and head shots.

6. Some meals while on assignments.

7. Agent's fees.

8. A home office.

There several other gray areas like entertainment, telephone bills, home office expenses, and the like. Try to find a tax accountant who is familiar with the entertainment field and save your receipts!

There are also other areas that a model should explore. Look at IRA accounts since you are not paying Social Security on most of your earnings. The key is to keep a good record of everything and keep your monthly expenses separated from your personal expenses.

Back to the amount of time and effort you spend in promoting your company – which is you. Look at the quality of your wares – which is also you. You can go out of business as easily as a 'burger joint if you do not manage your business affairs properly. While modeling seems to be a part-time endeavor, it should always be viewed as a profession and approached in a businesslike fashion.

A final order note on taxes. Recently, the IRS has attack artists who are not showing a consistent profit with their work. If you're not making a profit, even a marginal one, from your modeling it is possible the IRS may decide that your career is actually a hobby. In that case they may go back several years and disqualify all of your deductions. Therefore, it is advisable to manage your expenses wisely and to make sure that you are able to show a profit in at least one out of every three years.

# 8 DO IT

This cannot be counted as a tip in itself as it is something every model should know and be active in without being told. Such is not always the case unfortunately. Modeling is hard work. It involves a good bit of sales ability: both in selling products and in the model's ability to sell his or her talent to the prospective client. It is also fun. However, it takes a lot of effort to get the jobs that allow you, the model, to have three or four hours of fun in front of the camera.

If you do not take time to hit the streets several hours a week (preferably several hours a day) you'll be just another of the hundreds of people who call themselves models and are such in name only. You must look for the jobs until you are well enough known and well enough respected in your field for the jobs come looking for you.

Do not think that having an agent will get the job done for you, either. Without the tools (portfolio composites and head shots) an agent is worthless to you. He can describe you all day long to a perspective client and the client still has no idea how you look.

The agent needs photos to send out, if not his efforts are worthless. It is your responsibility to provide the tools you need, not the agent's.

Also, having an agent does not mean you can sit at home, prop your feet up, and wait for the agent find work for you. Unless the client (usually here we mean advertising agencies and casting directors) has met you, even a photograph means very little. Your composites only show the client how you look. They do not say anything about your personality and they will not get your name planted in the client's mind. That's your job. Only *you* can do it.

I have seen over and over that the girls who take the time to meet the casting people professionally are the ones who bring in the work.

With a small agency you might receive more personalized attention but there you are still only one of many. A good agent will divide his time equally on all of his talent and not show favoritism. That is the best way for an agent to operate. It also means that you only have your fair share of his efforts and no more. Ergo: you need to do most of the initial leg work and let your agent do the follow-up in the contact negotiations. That is, after all, his main job.

***Tip: Being in front of the camera may just be a part time job, but modeling takes full time commitment for success.***

No one is going to make you a star. *You* have to do it yourself. There's a lot of competition and you'll have to be the one to measure up to it; not your agent, not your mother, not your best friend: you. *You* have to do the work. *You* have to do it. Nobody else well. If *you* do not do it, it will not get done. *You* must develop the willpower and find the motivation to get the work done.

Of course, you have already started. By reading this booklet, you now have the tools and basic understanding you need to succeed. Now go do it!

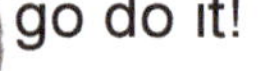

***Tip: Even though Gina was just barely over 5-foot tall and Hispanic, she was still a top earning model. Many times a casting call would specify tall, blonde, and blue-eyes... then they would ask for Gina by name. Why? Because she took the time to meet them personally.***

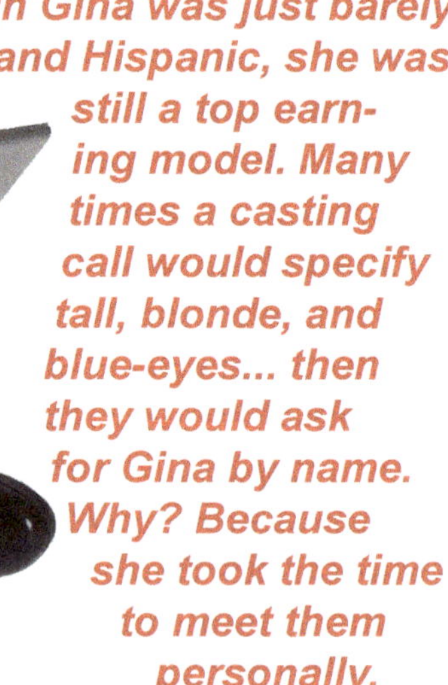

## Photo Credits

| Photographer | Source |
|---|---|
| Totti - Cover | / Dollar Photo Club |
| Janifest | / Dollar Photo Club |
| Masahito Mori | / Dollar Photo Club |
| Vladimir Voronin | / Dollar Photo Club |
| Aiwendyl | / Dollar Phoyo Club |
| Subbotina | / Deposit Photo |
| Katrina Brown | / Dollar Photo Club |
| Kassandra | / Dollar Photo Club |
| Alan Kasm | / Deposit Photo |
| Feedough | / Deposit Photo |
| Yeko Photo Studio | / Dollar Photo Club |
| Wavebreakmediamicro | / Dollar Photo Club |
| Wavebreakmedia Micro | / Dollar Photo Club |
| Sergey Bogdanov | / Dollar Photo Club |
| Snap2art (Postcard) | / Dollar Photo Club |
| Alexanderzam (Stamp) | / Dollar Photo Club |
| Dmvphotos (Flapper) | / Dollar Photo Club |
| Kanea | / Dollar Photo Club |
| Photobac (baby) | / Deposit Photo |
| Dml5050 (girl) | / Deposit Photo |
| Rob Byron | / Dollar Photo Club |
| Les Benton | / Les Benton |
| Arkusha | / Deposit Photo |
| Konradbak | / Deposit Photo |
| Syda Productions | / Dollar Photo Club |
| Everett225 | / Dollar Photo Club |
| ChenPG | / Dollar Photo Club |
| Egorrr | / Dollar Photo Club |
| Dxfoto.Com | / Dollar Photo Club |
| Alphaspirit | / Dollar Photo Club |
| Subbotina Anna | / Dollar Photo Club |

| Photographer | Source |
|---|---|
| Egorrr | / Deposit Photo |
| Piotr Marcinski | / Deposit Photo |
| Peter Atkins | / Dollar Photo Club |
| Sergeymalov | / Dollar Photo Club |
| Konradbak | / Deposit Photo |
| Syda Productions | / Deposit Photo |
| Konradbak | / Deposit Photo |
| Konradbak | / Deposit Photo |
| Olly18 | / Deposit Photo |
| Dashek | / Deposit Photo |
| Subbotina | / Deposit Photo |
| Stillkost | / Dollar Photo Club |
| Keeweeboy | / Deposit Photo |
| Fashion Stock | / Deposit Photo |
| Scott Griessel | / Dollar Photo Club |
| Focus Pocus , Ltd. | / Deposit Photo |
| Monkey Business | / Dollar Photo Club |
| Syda Productions | / Dollar Photo Club |
| Sergeymalov | / Dollar Photo Club |
| Matusciac | / Dollar Photo Club |
| Jin | / Dollar Photo Club |
| Akiyojo | / Dollar Photo Club |
| Pandorabox | / Dollar |
| Back Cover | Photo Club |

www.ingramcontent.com/pod-product-compliance
Ingram Content Group UK Ltd.
Pitfield, Milton Keynes, MK11 3LW, UK
UKHW062301290726
14090UKWH00017B/819